Community Links:
Pathways to Reconnection and Recovery

Program Implementation Manual

Mary Ellen Copeland, PhD
Shery Mead, MSW

Peach Press
Dummerston, Vermont

Copyright and Permission Information

Publishers Note

This publication is designed to provide accurate and authoritative information in regard to the subject matter covered. It is sold with the understanding that the publisher is not engaged in rendering psychological, financial, legal, or other professional services. If expert assistance or counseling is needed, the services of a competent professional should be sought.

Cover Design by Patti Smith

ISBN: 0-9631366-9-0

Printed in the United States of America

Published by Peach Press, P.O. Box 301, West Dummerston, VT 05357-0301

Peach Press Website address: www.mentalhealthrecovery.com

Table of Contents

Community Links:

Pathways to Reconnection and Recovery

Program Implementation Manual

Introduction

Community Links is a voluntary program that matches peers or community members with people who have (a) court orders of nonhospitalization or involuntary commitment, (b) are dependent on the mental health system for assistance and support, and/or (c) feel isolated from their community due to mental health difficulties. These peers or community members have been trained to assist and support others in developing positive reciprocal relationships, regaining their independence, integrating themselves into their community and improving the overall quality of their lives. The Community Links relationship diminishes over time as the person develops natural supports and becomes more comfortable in the community.

This program is based on the findings of the Moving Ahead Research Project (Shery Mead and Mary Ellen Copeland, coprincipal investigators, Vermont Real Choices Grant, 2004). In this qualitative research project, the researchers interviewed 28 people who were on orders of nonhospitalization or involuntary commitment. They found that people want to end their dependency on the mental health system, become more fully integrated into the community of their choice, develop the skills and strategies needed for independence and work toward meeting their own life dreams and goals. The Community Links Program was designed to meet his need. In designing the program, Copeland and Mead collaborated with:

- People who participated in the study;

- An advisory board that included people who have experienced mental health difficulties and who have had orders of involuntary commitment, people who have provided them with care and support, a representative from Vermont Protection and Advocacy, and a representative from the state-wide organization, Vermont Psychiatric Survivors;
- A committee from the funding agency, the Vermont State Department of Mental Health; and
- Research and program development consultants.

In addition, they reviewed programs from around the country that are designed to meet similar needs.

A Community Links pilot project was implemented in the late summer and fall of 2004 to test the project design. In this pilot project, 10 prospective Community Links were trained in three days of training. They were then matched with people who had contacted the program administrator requesting a Community Link. They had learned about the program through various project promotional efforts, including outreach to the state hospital facility and regional mental health centers. The Community Links and the person who requested the program, who will be called a "Linkee," worked together over an eight-week period, getting together once or twice a week for several hours.

The findings of the pilot project were used to revise the project design and develop this training manual in anticipation of:

1. Implementation of a Community Links program in Vermont, and
2. National distribution of the manual to facilitate replication in other regions.

This manual is a comprehensive guide to developing a Community Links program. However, given the wide variance in factors like need, capacity, population base, and regional and local ethnic and cultural differences, it is expected that the program will differ widely from place to place. To assure program adherence to Community Links values and ethics, and the ability to best meet the need, the program will need an effective coordinator, a supportive sponsoring agency, and an ongoing Working Committee of people committed to assuring a high quality program.

Program Goals

The goals of this program are to:

- Match people who have (a) court orders of nonhospitalization or involuntary commitment, (b) are dependent on the mental health system for assistance and support, and/or (c) feel isolated from their community due to mental health difficulties, with peers or community members who will assist and support them in regaining their independence, integrating themselves into their community, and improving the overall quality of their lives;
- Reduce the need for court orders of nonhospitalization and involuntary commitment, and dependence on the mental health system.

Who Are Community Links?

A Community Link can be anyone who:

- Enjoys being and working with others,
- Is generally self-confident and self-assured,
- Is willing to be self-critical,
- Is willing to learn and use the values and ethics of Community Links,

- Has either had personal success in developing connections with the community and some knowledge of available community resources, or is willing to learn this information and these skills, and
- Has several hours a week to be involved in this program.

Having life experience in the mental health system can be helpful but is not required. Being a Community Link gives a person an opportunity to enrich her/his own life while working closely with another person to facilitate recovery, independence and reintegration into the community. The position may be paid or voluntary, depending on the resources of the agency that sponsors the program.

Who Does Community Links Serve?

Community Links is for people who are dependent on the mental health system either with or without a court order, and who want to work toward interdependence, independence and community integration. This program is helpful to people who have been in institutions, lived in group homes or other kinds of care homes, or people whose mental health difficulties have kept them from participation in the community. Inclusion in the program may be dependent on funding and sponsoring agency stipulations. The only way a person can become involved in the Community Links program is through self-referral, although another person could make the contact for them as long as it is clear that the person really wants to be involved. The person will contact the Program Coordinator through a toll-free confidential phone line, mail or email. The sponsoring agency may set up some other system for making the contact. The Community Links relationship can be terminated at the request of the person who has requested the link.

How long does a Community Links relationship last?

The ideal is for the Community Link relationship to last as long as the person needs it. Many of the people who will be working with a Community Link have been disconnected from their community for many years and have little understanding of concepts like self-determination, empowerment, and natural supports. Therefore, they might benefit from having a Community Link for a long time, even years. However, this may not be possible given funding and program parameters. There may need to be a limitation on the amount of time the two people can work together, but six months would be the most effective minimum. In the pilot project of Community Links, due to funding issues and project timelines, people were matched with another person for only eight weeks. Even in that time period, by their own admission, people made remarkable progress in working toward their own goals of independence and community integration.

As the two people are working together, they are aware that the relationship as part of the Community Links program is time limited and that focus needs to be placed on self-determination and building community supports, gradually working to end the relationship or change it to friendship or peer support. Ongoing assessment by both people in the Community Links relationship, with the guidance of the Program Coordinator, will help them work toward a time when the Community Links relationship is no longer needed.

Program Administration

Agency or Organizational Sponsorship

The Community Links program is sponsored by an agency or organization that is responsible for:

- Program planning,
- Program implementation and administration, and
- Monitoring and evaluation.

Peer operated agencies and mental health organizations would be likely sponsors for this program. Traditional, medical or clinical mental health services would not be likely sponsors because they have reporting requirements that violate the confidentiality of this program. Every aspect of the Community Links program is voluntary. An individual must personally ask to be involved in the program. In the Moving Ahead study, the researchers found that people who have been involved in the mental health system for many years, and who have been coerced or feel like their power has been taken away, would not choose to be involved in a program that was part of the traditional mental health system where there would be reporting or analysis of their involvement, or where they would not be in charge of their involvement. They want their involvement in the program to be confidential. In Vermont, the program is sponsored by Vermont Psychiatric Survivors, a peer-run organization that sponsors recovery education initiatives and peer-support networking.

However, the sponsoring agency can work cooperatively with supporting agencies such as traditional mental health services and agencies, mental health centers, hospitals and institutions on program development, funding, promotion, recruitment and other aspects of the program to help ensure program success.

The sponsoring agency may be responsible for making major program decisions such as payment of the Program Coordinator, the Working Committee, and the Community Links; securing liability coverage for the length of Community Links relationships (hopefully six months or more when needed); numbers of trainings; and numbers of people that can be accommodated in the program.

Important

Reporting or analysis of participation is not allowed in this program. Findings of the Moving Ahead study show that reporting and analysis will interfere with willingness to participate and the effectiveness of the program. It violates the program ethics of empowerment, self-determination and confidentiality. The program <u>does not include</u> a system of reporting to anyone or analysis of individual participation. This includes agencies, agency staff, care providers and family members. Participant names will be confidential, known only by the Community Link and the Program Coordinator. The only reporting or assessment might be the voluntary sharing of nonpersonal information that could be used to assess program effectiveness like demographics, time spent together, and length of participation. A confidential qualitative assessment process or gathering of stories could be initiated if participants want to be involved.

Program Coordinator

The sponsoring agency hires a Program Coordinator to administer the program and to work with a Working Committee to carry out the tasks of the program. The Program Coordinator can be either a full-time or part-time person, depending on the size of the program. Although there are no specific educational requirements for this position, it is suggested that the Program

Coordinator have administrative and organizational experience as well as experience working in leadership roles in mental health recovery and peer-run programs. This person must be willing to learn about Community Links and to adhere to the values of the program. The ideal person would be innovative, creative, responsible, competent and flexible.

Working Committee

The Program Coordinator works with a committee of up five people to implement all aspects of the program. The Working Committee needs to include at least three people who have experience as users of mental health services. Ideally it would include people who have had or have involuntary commitment orders. These people need to have knowledge of mental health recovery and peer-run programs, be energetic, and be willing to work collaboratively on implementing Community Links.

Program Coordinator and Working Committee Tasks

The Program Coordinator and the Working Committee:

- Study the program manual,
- Set up a toll-free phone line, fax line, mailing address and email address,
- Recruit Training Leaders and prospective Community Links,
- Arrange and implement the Community Links training described in this manual,
- Promote Community Links as an option for people who feel they will benefit from this project,
- Respond to requests for a Community Link,
- Match people who might benefit from working together,
- Support Community Links as they work with the person with whom they are linked,
- Set up and maintain an ongoing system of program evaluation,

- Make program changes based on the program evaluation,
- Arrange or assist with transportation, and
- Provide additional activities and training based on the expressed needs of the Community Links or the people with whom they are linked.

The sponsoring agency, Program Coordinator and the Working Committee do not:

- Make direct referrals to the Community Links program,
- Provide therapeutic oversight, or
- Require progress or personal evaluative reports.

This project is based on the mental health recovery values of self-determination, personal empowerment and confidentiality. People who learn about the program and want a Community Link contact the Program Coordinator directly. Although an agency might suggest that a person would benefit from involvement in this program or inform them of the program, they cannot make a referral for this service.

Program Evaluation

The Program Coordinator is responsible for program monitoring and evaluation. She or he will work with the Working Committee, the Training Leaders, the Community Links and the people they are working with to provide ongoing assessment of the program for quality control, program improvement, and to collect information that can be used in reports for the sponsoring agency and funders. It is essential to maintain confidentiality and avoid judgment and analysis of program participants in all monitoring and evaluation activities.

The suggested evaluation tasks include:

Program Coordinator. The Program Coordinator will be responsible for ongoing program oversight, monitoring and evaluation. He or she will meet at least monthly, by phone or in person, with the Community Links and the person they are working with (three-way meetings) as a simple check-in and to assist in resolving possible difficulties.

Program Coordinator and Working Committee meetings. The Program Coordinator will be responsible for setting up regular meetings (weekly or every other week depending on the size of the program and current program activities) with the Working Committee. One person needs to be responsible for keeping detailed notes of these meetings for easy review and referral. They need to include records of ongoing program activity (how many Community Links are working, how many people are participating in the program, etc.), assessment, needed actions and improvements, any decisions made, who will implement tasks, and how and when these tasks will be completed.

Community Links as participants in the Community Links training. At the end of each of the first two sessions, the Training Leader will ask the participants for feedback on the day and to suggest possible changes for the next session. At the end of the last session, the Community Links will evaluate the training using the Community Links Evaluation Questions in Appendix C-14.

Training leaders. Following each day of the training, the Training Leaders will meet, review the day, address any issues raised by the participants, discuss difficult situations and suggestions for improvements, and make plans for implementing these changes. At the end of the training, they will review the evaluations from the participants and share these evaluations with the Program Coordinator. Working together, they can list suggestions that would improve the next training.

Community Links and the people they are working with. Both people in the Community Links relationship work together to answer the following questions. They can do it often, perhaps every other week. This will guide them in thinking about and recognizing how this program is working for both of them, help them plan future activities and make changes in the way they want to do things.

Community Links Evaluation Questions

1. How is this relationship working for you? What do you like about it? What would you like to change? How could we make that change in a way that would work well for both of us?
2. Are you sharing honestly how you feel in your Community Links relationship? If not, why not? How can we make it possible for you to share what you feel in this relationship? Are you asking for what you want and need? If not, why not? How can we make that possible?
3. What has changed about the way you think about things since the beginning of Community Links?
4. What do we need to do more of or less of to make sure that Community Links is working for both of us?

They can discuss these same questions with the Program Coordinator.

Stories

Stories are a rich way of collecting information that can be used to inform others of the program and support program activities. They should be collected whenever possible and stored where they can be easily accessed. A person on the Working Committee might be responsible for collecting program stories. To protect confidentiality, names and identifying information needs to be removed from the stories, and written permission needs to be secured from the person who told the story before it is shared.

Costs

The sponsoring agency in collaboration with the Program Coordinator and the Working Committee secure the funding to meet the cost of the program. Community Links is not an expensive program and can be implemented with limited funding if necessary. The major costs will be salaries or stipends for the Program Coordinator, members of the Working Committee, Training Leaders and Community Links. Community Links can be reimbursed for transportation and other costs. They need to know in advance what costs will be covered and how they will be reimbursed.

The Program Coordinator and the Working Committee can develop a program budget. In determining program costs, the following issues need to be considered:

- Payment for the Program Coordinator, the Working Committee, Training Leaders and Community Links;
- Promotional and recruitment materials;
- Office expenses like rent, equipment, supplies, phone and postage;
- Training costs (facility rental, lunches, travel, resources); and
- Funds to cover costs like transportation.

Community Links Program Promotion

Promotion is key to the success of this program. The goal of promotional efforts is to encourage people to (a) agree to be a Community Link, and (b) request a Community Link.

The Program Coordinator and the Working Committee develop and implement a promotional plan that they feel will be successful in their area. Promotional efforts need to be coordinated with the sponsoring agency or organization, other mental health organizations, and mental health treatment facilities, hospitals and institutions.

Promotion strategies

The following promotional strategies can be included in the promotion plan.

- Develop informational brochures, one-page handouts, posters, press releases and a press kit (information, press releases, related articles) that describe the program. (Include a toll-free number that people can call for information, to become a Community Link or to request a Community Link.)
- Distribute brochures, handouts and posters in places where people go who might be interested in this program, like mental health facilities, drop-in centers, soup kitchens and churches (see ideas for the poster in Appendix B-1).
- Hang posters in public places like grocery store bulletin boards, coffee shops, restaurants, public offices, drop in centers, and mental health facilities.
- Announce the program in the newspaper as a community news item, in church bulletins, and in newsletters, and particularly mental health newsletters.
- Announce and discuss the program on community talk radio shows and community access television.
- Meet with key people at places like mental health agencies, volunteer agencies, and senior centers to inform them of the program and to request their assistance in promotion.
- Leave applications to be a Community Link or to request a Community Link in places where people who might be interested congregate.

- Present to staff at mental health facilities and to patients at in-patient treatment centers, group homes, community care homes and institutions (see outline of promotional presentation in Appendix B-2).
- Hold well-advertised public informational meetings.
- Place articles in related newsletters and in the community newspapers.

The most important promotional tool will be informal networking between people who are involved in the program. Initial response to the program may be limited. As people become aware of the value of Community Links, and with continuing promotion and networking between participants, increased participation can be anticipated over time.

Becoming a Community Link

When potential Community Links express an interest in the program, they will be asked to fill out the application form that is included in Appendix B-3 and return it to the Program Coordinator. They could also be given the option of answering the questions on the form in a phone call or a personal meeting with the Program Coordinator.

Choosing Applicants to Participate in the Community Links Training

After the applications have been received, the Program Coordinator contacts all references, asking them if they feel this would be a good person to assist and support people in working toward mental health recovery, independence and community integration. If there are reservations about a person's appropriateness for the program, interview the applicant before deciding to include them in the Community Links training. The Program Coordinator and the Working Committee can work together to choose potential Community Links for the training. A consideration in making these choices may be choosing people they feel can best meet the needs of the people who have requested a Community Link. They may need to consider issues of diversity, including age, gender, sexual orientation, disability, and economic, educational, cultural and ethnic background, as they make these decisions.

People who have submitted applications need to be notified as soon as possible about their inclusion in the program and, if they are chosen for the training, given information about the training.

Requesting a Community Link

It will be difficult for many people to request a Community Link. It may be the first thing they have done on their own behalf in a very long time. They may be apprehensive and not trusting. They may procrastinate. When they finally make the call, or have someone make the call for them, they need to always be treated respectfully. In addition, to avoid discouragement, the match should be made as quickly as possible.

A person can request a Community Link by calling the toll-free number, by mail, email, fax, or by sending an application to the Program Coordinator. (This application is in Appendix B-4.)

The person requesting the Community Link should be given the option of answering the questions on the form by phone or in a meeting with the Program Coordinator. Remind the person that any information they share is confidential and will be used only by the Program Coordinator in deciding whom to match a person with. It will not be shared with any agency, organization, treatment facility or family member. Tell them when they can expect to hear details about the link.

Arranging the Match

When there are trained Community Links available and people who have requested links, the Program Coordinator, with the assistance of the Working Committee if necessary, decides who would be most likely to work well together. Same-sex matches are generally recommended. Other items that may or may not be issues to consider are:

- Convenience of location and transportation,
- Shared interests,
- Similar educational and cultural backgrounds,

- Age,
- Common experience,
- Special needs and accommodations, and
- Diversity (education, economic, cultural, ethnic, religion, gender, disability).

When decisions have been made about matches, arrange a time when the Community Link, the Linkee and the Program Coordinator can meet. This meeting can be held in the office of the Program Coordinator, but can be held elsewhere if that is more convenient for others. The Program Coordinator may need to assist the Linkee with transportation.

This meeting should be less than an hour long. Both the Community Link and Program Coordinator need to be aware that the Linkee may have difficulty trusting others and may be apprehensive. Therefore they will need to be understanding, patient, respectful, positive and, as always, nonjudgmental.

The Program Coordinator explains who she or he is and gives a one-sentence description of what they do. It might be, "I am Clyde Norman and I am responsible for all aspects of the Community Links Program." Then he or she introduces the Community Link to the person with whom they are being matched. The Program Coordinator might add something about the reason behind the match, for example, "I thought you would enjoy being together because you both like the outdoors and particularly enjoy fishing and watching sporting events."

The Program Coordinator reminds both people that all personal information shared in Community Links will not be shared with or reported to others, including mental health agencies and caseworkers.

The Program Coordinator asks the persons who are Community Links to share some things they would like the other person to know about them. Then the Linkee does the same thing. Hopefully this leads to conversation. If so, that's great.

Another topic that can be discussed at this initial meeting is what the Linkee considers "community" or would like to have as "community.". For instance, if a person has lived in a group home for a long time, that may be their community. What they are hoping for may be having friends outside of the group home and places they like to go and feel comfortable going in the community. They may want to move out of the group home and into their own apartment. Another person may live in his or her own home but spend little time with others and have no connection with the community. This person may want to be developing natural supports and getting out into the community from time to time.

The Program Coordinator explains that it is expected that the Community Link and the Linkee will work together rather intensively as they develop their relationship and work together. Over time, as the person becomes more comfortable in the community and develops some natural support, the amount of time spent together and the intensity of the relationship would diminish. Eventually the Community Link relationship will end but the two people involved can choose to remain friends and supporters. If, due to the parameters of the program as developed by the sponsoring agency or due to funding concerns, there is a time when the Community Link relationship must end, both people should be advised of this so they can plan accordingly.

The Program Coordinator asks if either of them have questions about the program. The Program Coordinator answers the questions. If the Program Coordinator doesn't know the answer to the questions, they can tell the person they will find out the answer and get back to them.

The Community Link and the Linkee can discuss issues like meeting places, transportation, and activities they might enjoy together. Before the meeting ends, they decide when and where they will meet next time and what they will do. A suggested activity is to use the Community Links listing of resources from the training and begin to work on a schedule of things they can do together. Information on subsequent meetings is included in the training.

If at this first meeting, it is clear that this is not a good match, people need to be honest with each other and share that concern. Then a different match can be arranged.

People Who Should Not Be a Community Link

During the training or during the initial meeting, it may become apparent to the Program Coordinator that a person is not appropriate to serve as a Community Link or to be in the Community Links program. Although it is a difficult task, the person must be gently told that they cannot be matched with a person and thanked for their time and interest. People requesting Community Links may have been badly treated in the mental health system and in their lives. Care must be given to assure that they are not badly treated in this program.

Working Together

In the training, the Community Link will learn how to work with the Linkee, teaching them recovery skills and strategies including developing a system of natural supports, assisting them in becoming integrated into their community and working toward meeting their own goals and dreams. At the beginning of the Community Links experience, it is anticipated that the relationship will be more intense. Over time, the relationship would become less intense as the person develops and uses new skills and becomes more comfortable in the community. At a mutually agreed upon time, the formal relationship between the Community Link and Linkee would end. However, the Community Link and the Linkee can continue to be friends or supporters if they want to do so.

Hopefully, Community Links will become an ongoing program. At any given time there will be people in Community Links who have been working together for several months and may be ending their relationship, and others who are just beginning to work together.

Program Monitoring and Evaluation

The Community Links program will benefit from ongoing monitoring and evaluation by the people in the Community Link relationship (the Community Link and the Linkee) in collaboration with the Program Coordinator and perhaps members of the Working Committee.

The Community Link and the Linkee need to check in with each other at each session. They need to ask each other:

- How are things going for you?
- How is this helping you?
- What are you learning?
- What do you like best about our time together?
- Is there anything you would like to change?
- Is there anything you need in this relationship?
- What has changed for you since we began doing this together?

Optional: One of the people can keep notes on their answers and any changes they want to make.

The Program Coordinator sets up regular meetings with the Community Link and the Linkee as it seems necessary. For convenience, these meetings can be held on the phone. The Program Coordinator keeps notes on responses. They discuss the same questions that the

Community Link and the Linkee ask each other each time they get together. The Program Coordinator keeps confidential notes on these meetings (name references and any personal information is left out or deleted). The Program Coordinator and the Working Committee review the notes from meetings and, if necessary, make changes in the program. They also use these notes as an ongoing record of the program.

It would be helpful to the sponsoring agency, the Program Coordinator, the Working Committee, Community Links, people who are interested in having a Community Link and others who are considering replicating this program if people involved in the program write or tape **stories** about their involvement in the program. If they are willing, these stories without the names, can be used in newsletters, promotional materials, reports, and funding requests. The Program Coordinator, a member of the Working Committee or a volunteer can be responsible for collecting these stories. It is imperative that, in collecting and using these stories, the confidentiality of both the Community Link and the person they are supporting is honored. Names, places, and identifying circumstances need to be deleted or changed. Before publishing anything about another person, show them exactly what you plan to publish and get their written permission. *If they are at all uncomfortable with what is said or how it is being used, do not use it.*

Community Links Training

Training Goal

The goal of the training is to prepare people to be Community Links. It will do this by:

- ☐ Defining the issue that the program addresses,
- ☐ Describing Community Links and the role of the Community Link,
- ☐ Developing a Community Links Wellness Recovery Action Plan,
- ☐ Describing the personal WRAP process and how to use it in Community Links,
- ☐ Practicing finding resources in the community,
- ☐ Thinking about community and what it means to people engaged in this program,
- ☐ Discussing help in the Community Links relationship,
- ☐ Introducing language that promotes recovery and community integration,
- ☐ Exploring ways to build trusting and mutually supportive relationships,
- ☐ Learning to negotiate in relationships,
- ☐ Learning and practicing listening skills,
- ☐ Discussing and practicing first contact, working together and ending the Community Links relationship,
- ☐ Working on understanding rights and responsibilities in the relationship and in the community,
- Learning and practicing Community Links values, and
- Describing Community Links evaluation, monitoring and protocols.

Arranging the Training

The Program Coordinator and the Working Committee set up the Community Link training. This training is designed to be held for three days from 9 AM to 4:30 PM. However, a different schedule could be used that includes all of the training modules. For instance, the training could be held on six half days or evenings. The Program Coordinator and the Working Committee could also set up additional training sessions for Community Links after the initial training, while people are in their Community Links relationships. The topics for these additional sessions would be based on the needs of the Community Links.

It is recommended that the training be held on nonconsecutive days to allow time between each training day for participants to assimilate their learning and to complete assignments. It will also be important to have the training days fairly close together so trainees can build on what they learned at the previous session. For instance, the training could be on Tuesday and Friday of one week and Tuesday of the next week. This may also make it easier for some people to attend who cannot easily get away for consecutive days.

Each training day will be divided into four 1.5-hour modules with 15-minute breaks in the morning and afternoon and an hour break for lunch. The day will end with a half-hour period of reflection on the day.

Location, Meals, Snacks, Beverages, Transportation

The training needs to be held in a convenient location that is easily accessible, with comfortable seating, windows, ample room for at least 15 people to meet together, preferably sitting around tables, and space for small group meetings.

If possible, snacks, lunch, and beverages can be provided. Snacks like popcorn, cheese and crackers, a vegetable platter and/or fresh fruit are always appreciated. A simple healthy lunch of pizza or some kind of ethnic take out is a pleasant reward for the participants. If necessary, participants can be asked to bring a bag lunch. Foods that are high in sugar, salt or fat like candy, donuts, pastries or cakes may make participants drowsy and can be avoided. Beverages need to be available at all times. Water can be on the tables in bottles or pitchers with cups for each person, or it could be available from a water cooler or at the table where the snacks are served. People also appreciate having coffee, decaffeinated coffee, tea, a selection of herbal teas and fruit juice available through the day. Soda might be available for purchase through a soda machine or participants who want it can be asked to bring their own. Costs for provided snacks, meals, beverages, and transportation to the training are generally paid for by the sponsoring organization.

Training Leaders

The Program Coordinator and the Working Committee decide on at least two people who are willing and best suited to lead the Community Links training. These are usually people who have been doing mental health recovery and peer-support work for some time, and are recognized for their training and leadership skills. The Training Leaders can be the Program Coordinator and members of the Working Committee. If possible, at least one of the Training Leaders should be a person who has experience as a user of mental health services to ensure that this perspective is represented. If there is no one available who has this experience, you may want to have one or several people with that experience assist at the first training and subsequent trainings, preparing them to lead the training as soon as they feel ready to do so. It is also helpful if at least one of the Training Leaders has past experience in teaching and training.

The three days of training are implemented by the Program Coordinator, the Working Committee and the Training Leaders. In advance of the training, they need to work together, carefully studying this manual, developing plans for the training, making necessary arrangements, and gathering needed resources.

Participants

The training participants are approximately 10 people who have an interest in becoming Community Links. They may be people who have experience in the mental health system, have court-ordered treatment or hospitalization, are family or care providers, or are members of the community. If necessary, this training could easily be adapted to train fewer people. For instance, if five Community Links are needed in a rural area, the training can be adapted to meet this need. However, since this is an intensive training, it is not recommended for more than 10 people. If you have more people who need to be trained, schedule an additional training. Several other people might attend the training in addition to the Training Leaders to provide assistance during the training, including typing and printing of notes to be used as handouts. These could be members of the Working Committee, the Program Coordinator, and people who would like to eventually become Training Leaders.

Depending on the comfort of the Training Leaders, several interested people could attend the training as observers. These might be people who are considering sponsoring a training or who have some other interest in understanding the program. This needs to be planned in advance and these observers need to be introduced to the participants with a brief explanation of why they are there.

Everyone who attends the training, the participants who will become Community Links, the Training Leaders and Working Committee, assistants and observers, needs to follow the Participant Guidelines developed by the participants in the first module of the training.

Advance Tasks for the Program Coordinator, Working Committee, and Training Leaders

In anticipation of the training, the Program Coordinator, the Working Committee and the Training Leaders, will work together to:

- ☐ Plan the training, following the instructions in this manual. This is a very time consuming task and needs focused attention.
- ☐ To inform your thinking, read the articles in Section A of the Appendix.
- ☐ Recruit prospective Community Links (and if necessary, people who want to work with a Community Link).
- ☐ Secure a place to hold the training and arrange for snacks, beverages and meals.
- ☐ Advise participants of the details of the training.
- ☐ Arrange transportation and transportation reimbursement if necessary.
- ☐ Arrange for a computer, digital projector and screen for the PowerPoint slides or an overhead projector if you make copies of transparencies from the CD.
- ☐ Purchase training resources and supplies including (a) binders with a set of four tabs for each training participant where they can keep notes and that have room to include information they will need during the training; and (b) binders or accordion envelopes that participants can give the person they are linked with that they can use to keep their contact schedule and information on resources in the community.
- ☐ Put together a binder for each participant in the training including information on Community Links protocols. Refer to the section *Participant Binders* for further information.

- ☐ Arrange to have a computer and printer with binder paper available throughout the training for making copies of notes, and ask one or several people to share responsibility for typing the notes and making them into handouts.

Activity Descriptions

There are several different kinds of activities included in this training. Descriptions of these activities follow:

Presentation

There will be times when a Training Leader introduces a topic or shares specific information with the group in a brief verbal presentation. Before making such a presentation, the Training Leader needs to know the information to be presented, having studied it in advance. *The presentation should be as brief as possible, summarizing the material with some, but not too much, supporting information.* Key points can be illustrated through writing them on a sheet of easel-pad paper or by making a transparency. Allow time for further information sharing and questions. Refer people to related handouts in their binder.

Discussion

Discussion is group conversation about a specific topic or issue. It can happen in small or larger groups. The Training Leader introduces the topic or asks the group a question. Then together, through dialogue with everyone in the group, they work together to find possible answers to the question and uncover new and different ways of thinking. Discussion can help people assess, and sometimes change or expand their thinking on specific topics. It helps to have some guidelines about how long people can talk. The group could also have the rule that no one talks a second time until everyone that wants to has had a chance to speak. One person could write the key points on a sheet of easel-pad paper.

Easel-pad Note Taking

The participants can respond to questions and requests for group input by generating lists. These lists can be recorded on easel paper by a Training Leader or a volunteer from the group. Label the sheet of paper with the topic that is being addressed. Print responses in large print and as clearly as possible using dark colored markers. Use extra sheets of easel paper as needed. Various colors of dark magic markers make them easy to read, give emphasis and differentiate one response from the next. Post the completed sheets on the wall.

Using the easel-pad paper that is sticky across the top of the back facilitates posting. However, this is much more expensive. You can easily use the easel-pad paper that doesn't stick and attach the sheets to the wall with tape.

Responses can be typed into a computer and copies can be made into a handout to give to participants at the next session. It is very empowering for people to see their thoughts recorded. To have it written makes it even more significant. And to have it typed and given out as a handout makes it even more powerful.

Easel-pad note taking can also be used in small groups. The group would meet to discuss a particular topic or question. They would then write or draw their response on one or several sheets of easel paper. It could be posted in the room and participants could have an opportunity to share their response with the rest of the group.

PowerPoint Presentation or Transparencies

- This manual includes a CD-ROM that has a PowerPoint presentation of slides to accompany many of the training modules. There will be instructions with each module that include the numbers of the slides to use with that module. You will need a screen for showing the slides if you use a data projector or an overhead projector.

- To use the slides from the CD you will need a laptop computer and a data projector. The sponsoring organization may have one, one could be borrowed from another organization, or the equipment could be rented. If you are going to use this system, try it in advance to make sure it works.
- Another option is to make transparencies and show them with an overhead projector. You can print the transparencies from your computer on transparency paper. This is the cheapest option. You could also print the transparencies on paper and have them copied as transparencies at a copy shop. However, this can be quite expensive.
- If you don't have access to either of these options, you could write the information on sheets of easel-pad paper.
- The participants will have copies of all the transparencies as thumbnail sketches in their binder. They could follow along as you read the key points.

Small Groups

There are several modules where it is suggested that the participants divide into small groups for a specified period of time to discuss a particular topic. This program is designed for people to divide into groups of three. However, if you have 10 people at the training or a number not divisible by three, Training Leaders or observers can be in the small groups. One person in the group records the general responses from the group and reports back to the larger group when they reconvene. After the person reports to the larger group, people in the reporting group need to have the opportunity to add other comments.

Problem Solving

In a problem-solving activity, a participant suggests a possible problem. This problem is written across the top of a sheet of easel-pad paper and underneath that are written the words "possible solutions." The members of the group give suggestions for solving the problem. These suggestions are listed on the easel pad (see Easel-pad Note Taking). The person who suggested the problem does not interrupt with reasons why the solution would work or why it would not work. After the group has generated a list of possible solutions, the easel-pad sheet is given to the person who had the problem so they can consider the various solutions later. Then another person has an opportunity to share a problem.

Graduations/Celebrations

On the last day of the training, or at some time during the training, participants can plan a celebration. This includes certificates of recognition for each participants and can include special refreshments (cake, ice cream, pizza, etc.), balloons, a flower or small token for each person, etc. If time allows, each participant can have an opportunity to talk to the group about their achievement.

Participant Binders

The Training Leaders work with the Program Coordinator and the Working Committee to put together a binder for each participant before the training: A sturdy binder with pockets inside the front and back and a set of four tabs is suggested. Identifying labels can easily be printed on the computer. If the book Wellness Recovery Action Plan has been purchased for each participant, the book can be placed in the front inside pocket. A copy of the Community Links Agenda Overview (Appendix C-1) is inserted in the front of the manual. The following sections can be written on the tabs and filled with copies from this manual and resources from the community:

- **Community Links Protocols**: These documents need to be developed by the Program Coordinator and the Working Committee. It addresses the issues discussed in Day 3, Module 2 of the Training, stipends, reimbursements, liability coverage, timelines, the initial meeting, reporting and evaluation, and stories.

- **Training handouts**: These are included in Appendix C and need to be copied prior to the training and inserted in the binder.
- **Handouts**: These are developed during the training.
- **Transparencies**: Thumbnail sketches of all the transparencies used in the training (copy from Appendix C-2).
- **Resources**: A section to insert information on resources the Community Link discovers in the Community (these may need to be punched with a three hole punch for ease of inclusion).

Prior to the Training

At least two weeks before the training, participants are sent an informational packet that includes specific information about the training (location, travel arrangements, meals), and the training agenda.

Starting and Ending Time, Breaks

The training starts at 9 AM unless other arrangements have been made. It begins with 15 minutes of check-in and review of housekeeping details. The day is divided into four modules that are 1.5-hours long. Each day includes a 15-minute break in the morning, a 15-minute break in the afternoon, a 45-minute break for lunch and time for reflections at the end of the day.

Training Guidelines

In module 1 on the first day of the training, the group will work together to develop Participant Guidelines that will help promote a successful training. These guidelines should be followed closely. If an issue comes up in the group that is not covered in the guidelines, such as people talking while other people are talking or talking out of turn, the Training Leader or a participant can suggest a new guideline to address that topic.

If the group is not following the guidelines, a Training Leader can remind them to do so. If a person does not follow the guidelines, a Training Leader can remind that person to follow the guidelines during a break, referring to the specific guideline in question.

Sometimes there will be unanticipated issues that make it difficult for the group to work together. If this occurs, the Training Leader or a person in the group can bring this to the attention of the rest of the group. The group can discuss the issue and decide how to resolve it. If it involves a specific person or a group of people, it is important within the context of this training to address the issue openly and honestly. Very occasionally it may be necessary to ask a person to leave the group. Possible reasons might be sexual harassment or stigmatizing behavior. If this has to be done, it can be done gently and firmly, in a way that causes the least possible disruption to the group.

In order to cover all of the information in the training, the Training Leaders will have to adhere closely to the suggested timelines. It is also important to give each participant time to share their thoughts with the group. It can be difficult to maintain this balance. The Training Leaders can work together to meet this challenge. This problem can be worsened if one or several people in the group talk more often than others, or talk too much. If this becomes an issue in the group, the Training Leaders may want to decide how long each person can share, for instance 2 to 3 minutes, and then use a timer or a clock to time responses. Also, everyone in the group who wants to speak needs to be given the chance to speak before anyone is given a second speaking opportunity. The Training Leaders may have to end the discussion by saying, "We have to move on now."

Agenda Overview

The following overview of the training agenda is included at the front of the Participant Manual. There is a copy of it in Appendix C-1 for ease of copying.

Day 1

8:45–9:00 Housekeeping

9:00–10:30 Module 1

- Introductions
- Participant guidelines
- Defining the issue

10:30–10:45 Break

10:45–12:15 Module 2

- Describing Community Links and the role of Community Links

12:15–1:00 Lunch

1:00–2:30 Module 3

- Developing a Community Links Wellness Recovery Action Plan

2:30–2:45 Break

2:45–4:15 Module 4

- Developing a Community Links Wellness Recovery Action Plan (continued)
- Description of personal WRAP process and how to use it in Community Links

4:15–4:30

- Reflections on the day and assignment for the next session

Day 2

8:45–9:00 Housekeeping

9:15–10:30 Module 1

- Sharing community resources
- Thinking about community
- Helping in the Community Links relationship

10:30–10:45 Break

10:45–12:15 Module 2

- Using language that promotes recovery and community integration
- Building trusting and mutually supportive relationships
- Negotiating the relationship

12:15–1:00 Lunch

1:00–2:30 Module 3

- Listening skills
- Listening practice

2:30–2:45 Break

2:45–4:15 Module 4

- First Contact
- Advocacy, rights and responsibilities

4:15–4:30

- Reflections on the day

Assignment—Returning to the community to discover more resources.

Day 3

8:45–9:00 Housekeeping

9:00–10:30 Module 1

- Getting together
- Gradually reducing the Community Link relationship

10:30–10:45 Break

10:45–12:15 Module 2

- Community Links values
- Values in action
- How do we know Community Links is working

12:15–1:00 Lunch

1:00–2:30 Module 3

- Report on community resources
- Community Links protocols

2:30–2:45 Break

2:45–4:00 Module 4

- Group problem solving

4:00–4:30

- Reflections on the training and celebration

Training Content

DAY 1

The Training Leaders arrive at least one-half hour early to make preparations for the day and so they can:

- Greet the participants as they arrive,
- Give them a copy of the Community Links Participant Manual,
- Ask them to make a name tag with first name in large bold letters,
- Show them to the meeting room.

Housekeeping (15 minutes)

Goal: To acquaint people with the training agenda, general program policies and the training facility.

Refer participants to the training agenda at the front of their manual. Share the following information:

- Starting and ending time,
- Breaks and lunch times,
- Availability of snacks, lunch and beverages,
- How to find the rest rooms,
- Smoking regulations,
- How to leave the building if there is an emergency and where to gather outside,

- Telephone access, and
- Cell phone policy (consider asking participants to keep cell phones off unless they might need to hear from children or other dependents—in that case they should leave the training room to talk if they get a call).

Module 1

Introductions (40 minutes)

Goal: To help people get to know each other and feel at ease in the group.

The Training Leaders briefly introduce themselves to the group (5 minutes or less each). The introduction is an opportunity for the participants to get to know the Training Leader and to help the participants feel at ease in the training. In the introduction, the Training Leader can share:

- Their name, the town they are from,
- Highlights of their history or life, or a short story that might be of interest, and
- Why they are doing this work.

The Participants introduce themselves by sharing their name, a reason why they want to be a Community Link and something the other members of the group might like to know about them. Other people who are attending the group should also introduce themselves at this time and explain why they are attending (to learn more about the program, to learn how to be a Training Leader, they are on the Working Committee, etc.).

Participant Guidelines (15 minutes)

Goal: To develop a list of guidelines for Training Leaders, participants and anyone else who is attending the training that will help ensure a comfortable and safe learning environment.

A Training Leader writes Participant Guidelines across the top of a sheet of easel-pad paper. The Training Leader then asks everyone who will be attending to share what they need to feel comfortable and safe in the training. If few people offer suggestions, the Training Leader can share ideas and the group can decide if they want these ideas added to the list. Some things that might be included on the list would be:

- Confidentiality of any personal information,
- Treating each other with dignity, compassion and respect,
- Avoiding judgments, teasing and "put-downs,"
- Avoiding interrupting when others are speaking,
- Taking care of personal needs,
- Keeping remarks brief so everyone gets a chance to share,
- Returning from breaks on time, and
- Starting and ending at the agreed upon times.

These guidelines can be amended at any time during the training if requested by the participants and all participants agree on the amendment.

Defining the Issue (20 minutes)

Goal: To describe the problem that this program addresses.

Using transparencies/slides 2 and 3 as a guide, a Training Leader describes the problem that the Community Links program is addressing.

Transparency content:

Defining the Issue. Although many people who have experienced mental health difficulties are recovering and moving on with their lives, there are many people who:

- Have lost hope and their ability to self-advocate,
- Have stopped working toward meeting their life goals and dreams,
- Are treated badly and/or stigmatized by others,
- Have become separated and ostracized from their natural supports and their community,
- Seem stuck in the mental health system,
- Are dependent on the mental health system for most or all aspects of their daily lives,
- May have had repeated commitment orders or a court order that limits their freedom and may include involuntary hospitalization and forced treatment,
- May live in a group home, supported housing or community care facility or an institution, or
- Don't have a home.

What do people in this circumstance want? (transparencies/slides 4 and 5)

The Moving Ahead study showed that these people want:

- To be treated well.

- To feel accepted in their families.
- To have friends and supporters outside of the mental health system.
- To be a part of their community.
- To learn to use mental health recovery skills and strategies.
- To have recovery security so they can recover without fear of losing benefits and services.
- To be able to do the things they like to do.
- To work toward their own goals and dreams.

Module 2

Describing Community Links and the Role of the Community Link

Goal: To describe the Community Links program and the role of the Community Link.

Using transparencies/slides 6 to 16 as a guide, the Training Leader

1. Reads the transparencies about each topic to the group,
2. Asks participants if they have any questions or concerns about that topic, and
3. Asks the participants for other ideas that might be included on that list, writing these ideas on a sheet of easel-pad paper.

These additional items are developed into a handout to be given out at the next session.

The Community Link and the Person They Are Working With (20 minutes)

- Connect and build reciprocal relationships where they can learn and grow together,
- Model the kinds of relationships that people would have in the community,

- ☐ Learn their strengths and use these strengths to link with activities and people in the community,
- ☐ Talk openly about what each of them needs in the relationship, like honesty, mutuality, and respect,
- ☐ Accept each other as they are,
- ☐ Focus on strengths, possibilities and successes,
- ☐ Are clear about expectations like being on time, being in contact if appointments can't be kept, and respecting agreed upon boundaries,
- ☐ Discuss and respect each person's boundaries,
- ☐ Keep personal information confidential,
- ☐ Share difficult times they have had, along with details of how they resolved the situations,
- ☐ Decide how to handle difficult situations that may arise,
- ☐ Set up a schedule of things they can do together (or decide after each visit what they will do the next time),
- ☐ Discover resources in the community that might be fun, interesting or helpful,
- ☐ Work on developing a system of natural supports,
- ☐ Attend meetings, groups and workshops together,
- ☐ Work on developing personal Wellness Recovery Action Plans or a Wellness Recovery Action Plan for their relationship,
- ☐ Evaluate their relationship,
- ☐ Assist with overall program monitoring and evaluation, and

- Work gradually toward a time when the Community Link is no longer needed in that role, and the person has natural supports and feels comfortable in the community.

What Community Links Do (20 minutes)

- LISTEN,
- Assist and support the other person in making personal decisions,
- Offer ideas and suggestions,
- Point out the other person's strengths,
- Remind the other person that there is no limit to what they can do,
- Remind the other person that they have the right to work toward their own goals and dreams,
- Share simple, safe things a person can do to feel well and to get through difficult times,
- Work with the other person on developing a personal Wellness Recovery Action Plan,
- Assist the person in developing a circle of natural supports and feeling comfortable in the community,
- Treat the other person in ways that make her or him feel respected,
- Reach out for assistance and support from the Program Coordinator, and
- Work toward a time when the person no longer needs the Community Links relationship (they may still be friends and even mutual supporters).

Community Links Don't Do (20 minutes)

- Try to be, or act like, experts,

- ☐ Tell the other person what to do,
- ☐ Judge, evaluate, or try to analyze the other person,
- ☐ Focus on problems and illness,
- ☐ Make assumptions about the other person,
- ☐ Violate the other person's boundaries,
- ☐ Loan the other person money or things,
- ☐ Get into an intimate or sexual relationship with each other,
- ☐ Meet in bars,
- ☐ Use coercion or threats,
- ☐ Do anything that violates a court order,
- ☐ Talk about each other behind the other person's back, or
- ☐ Report specifics of their Community Links relationship to any agency, care provider, family member or other supporter.

"If Community Links Works for You, What Will Be different in Your Life?" (15 minutes)

Goal: To help people think more deeply about what participation in this program will mean to them. Each participant is asked to share what they think will be different in their life if this program works for them. Responses are recorded and given as a handout.

Module 3

Developing a Community Links Wellness Recovery Action Plan

The Community Links Toolbox: A Community Links Wellness Toolbox (20 minutes)

Goal: To help participants become aware of the many resources they can use in their Community Links relationship, and to develop a Community Links Wellness Recovery Action Plan. Participants can refer to the Wellness Recover Action Plan Overview in Appendix C-3 and the sample Wellness Recovery Action Plan for the Community Link relationship. There is also a description of Peer Counseling Appendix C-4.

Using transparency/slide 17 as a guide, describe the Wellness Recovery Action Plan process.

Transparency content:

Wellness Recovery Action Plan

- ☐ Wellness Toolbox,
- ☐ Daily Maintenance Plan,
- ☐ What I'm like when I feel well,
- ☐ What I need to do every day to feel well,
- ☐ Things I might need to do to feel well,
- ☐ Triggers and a Triggers Action Plan,
- ☐ Early Warning Signs and an Early Warning Signs Action Plan,
- ☐ When Things are Breaking Down and an Action Plan,
- ☐ Crisis Plan, and

- Post Crisis Plan.

The Training Leader shares the list of skills and tools (Community Links Wellness Toolbox, transparencies/slides 18-21) that can be used to help the participants understand the kinds of things that might be possible. Group members share other ideas for things that can be included in this toolbox. These ideas are recorded on a sheet of easel-pad paper and made into a handout for the next session. Refer participants to the Capacity Inventory, Appendix C-11, for other ideas on possible Wellness Tools and things they can do together.

Community Links Wellness Toolbox:

- Validating the other person's experiences
- Being honest with each other
- Having open discussion of an issue
- Doing something fun together
- Doing something together that neither of you have ever done
- Participating in peer counseling
- Giving the other person listening time
- Discussing a topic of mutual concern
- Staying present in the situation
- Taking a break from the relationship
- Making a schedule
- Revising the schedule
- Spending more time together
- Spending less time together
- Arranging calls between the times you get together

- ☐ Searching for new community resources
- ☐ Going to an event in the community together
- ☐ Attending a support group together
- ☐ Attending a meeting of a special interest group
- ☐ Checking out the newspaper Community Calendar listings

What Would a Community Links Relationship Be Like If It Was Going Well? (20 minutes)

Goal: To clarify a good Community Links relationship.

A Training Leader reviews the following list (transparency/slides 22 and 23) and asks the group to share other ideas. These ideas are written on a sheet of easel-pad paper and developed into a handout to be given out at the next session.

Transparency content:

Community Links Relationship is Going Well:

- ☐ Both participants feel satisfied with the relationship.
- ☐ The participants feel comfortable being together.
- ☐ Participants look forward to spending time together.
- ☐ People can take risks together.
- ☐ People challenge each other.
- ☐ Neither person has more power than the other person.
- ☐ There is easy conversation.
- ☐ The relationship is fun.

Things to Do Each Time You Get Together to Keep the Relationship Going Well: (15 minutes)

Goal: To understand what needs to stay the same at each session to ensure a healthy relationship.

A Training Leader reviews the following lists (transparency/slide 24) and asks the group to share other ideas. These ideas are written on a sheet of easel pad paper and developed into a handout to be given out at the next session.

Transparency content:

Things to do each time you get together:

- ☐ Have a comfortable place to meet.
- ☐ Arrive on time.
- ☐ Spend a few minutes at the beginning of the time together talking about things that have happened recently and getting reacquainted.
- ☐ Decide if what you had planned to do is what you really need and want to do.
- ☐ Review and respond to the evaluation questions.
- ☐ Make a plan for the next time you will get together.

Choices of Things You Can Do When You Get Together: (20 minutes)

Goal: To introduce participants to the many possible activities that they can do with the person they are linked with.

A Training Leader reviews the following list (transparencies/slides 25 and 26) and asks the group to share other ideas. These ideas are written on a sheet of easel-pad paper and developed into a handout to be given out at the next session. Refer them to the Capacity Inventory, Appendix C-11 for other ideas on Wellness Tools and things they can do together.

Transparency content:

Things you can do when you get together:

- ☐ Peer counsel.
- ☐ Have a conversation.
- ☐ Listen.
- ☐ Make a list of Wellness Tools.
- ☐ Work on a Wellness Recovery Action Plan.
- ☐ Go to a restaurant for a cup of coffee.
- ☐ Talk about work possibilities.
- ☐ Visit a possible job site.
- ☐ Go to the local senior center.
- ☐ Attend a support group.
- ☐ Go to an exercise class.
- ☐ Go to a movie or a concert.
- ☐ Go to the library.
- ☐ Shop.
- ☐ Organize.
- ☐ Get together with several other people.
- ☐ Make a list of places in the community you would like to visit together.
- ☐ Pay bills.
- ☐ Make appointments.

Module 4

Wellness Recovery Action Plan for Community Links (cont.)

What Things Could Happen in Your Lives or in the Community That Could Affect the Community Links Relationship (15 minutes)

Goal: To help participants think about difficult times that might come up and how they can use some of the tools to address these difficulties.

A Training Leader reviews the following lists (transparencies/slides 27 and 28) and asks the group to share other ideas. These ideas are written on a sheet of easel-pad paper and developed into a handout to be given out at the next session.

Transparency content:

Things that could happen in your lives or the community that might affect the Community Links relationship:

- A time together is missed because of bad weather,
- A person is having difficulty with benefits,
- You visit a place together and are treated badly,
- The two of you have a misunderstanding,
- One of you forgets an appointment you had with each other,
- You can't do something you had planned because your car breaks down,
- One of you has a tragedy in your family,
- One of you has an accident or a serious illness,
- A horrible thing happens in your community, or
- A horrible thing happens in the world.

Community Links Wellness Tools you could use to get through this difficult time transparency/slide 29):

- ☐ Talk on the phone.
- ☐ Spend lots of time talking.
- ☐ Do peer counseling.
- ☐ Spend extra time together.
- ☐ Arrange to meet at another time.
- ☐ Review your wellness tools and choose to do several of them.
- ☐ Discuss the situation with the Program Coordinator.
- ☐ Give yourselves a treat.
- ☐ Cook some food or a meal for the other person.

Early Warning Signs That the Relationship Isn't Going Well (15 minutes)

Goal: To help participants think about signs that the relationship isn't going well, and provide wellness tools they could use to improve the relationship.

A Training Leader reviews the following list (transparencies/slides 30 and 31) and asks the group to share other ideas. These ideas are written on a sheet of easel-pad paper and developed into a handout to be given out at the next session.

Transparency content:

Early warning signs that the relationship isn't going well:

- ☐ The person cancels each time you agreed to be together.
- ☐ It's hard to find things to say to each other.
- ☐ The two of you can't think of anything you'd like to do together.

- It feels like a chore to get together.
- The relationship feels uncomfortable to one or both of you.
- One or both of you are beginning to think of ending the relationship.
- After you leave your time together you feel badly.

Tools you could use if either of you notice early warning signs (transparency/slide 32):

- Talk openly about what is happening and see if you can come up with some ideas of what to do about it.
- Change your plans.
- Get together less often or more often.
- Go to a movie or a concert.
- Watch a video together.
- Do peer counseling.
- Make some food together and eat it.
- Change your plans.
- Discuss the situation with the Program Coordinator.

The Community Links Relationship Is Going Badly (15 minutes)

Goal: To help participants recognize when the relationship is going badly or things are going badly in the life of the Linkee, and to take some positive action to improve and/or save the relationship.

A Training Leader reviews the following list (transparency/slide 33) and asks the group to share other ideas. These ideas are written on a sheet of easel-pad paper and developed into a handout to be given out at the next session.

Transparency content:

The Community Links relationship is going badly:

- One of you wants to end the relationship.
- There is a lack of trust.
- One of you is having mental health difficulties.
- One of you is in the hospital.
- One of you is overmedicated and is sleeping during your time together.
- You are being rude to each other.

Tools you could use to improve or save the relationship if things are going badly (transparency/slide 34 and 35):

- Spend time listening to the other person without giving advice or judging.
- Discuss the situation openly.
- Do peer counseling.
- Ask the person what you can do to help.
- Ask them what has happened.
- Ask the other person what needs to change and see if that change is possible.
- Talk to the Program Coordinator.
- End the relationship (the person might be matched with someone else).
- Call or visit the person if they are in the hospital .

Description of Personal WRAP Process and How to Use It in Community Links (30 minutes)

Goal: Introduce people to the strategy of working with their link on a personal Wellness Recovery Action Plan.

Distribute copies of the book Wellness Recovery Action Plan book or direct them to the handout describing WRAP in their manual. Using transparency/slide 36, a Training Leader describes the personal WRAP process, asking participants to share examples as he or she proceeds. Refer them to the Wellness Recovery Action Plan: Personal WRAP Overview, Appendix C-3, or, if they have a copy, to the book in the front of their manual, Wellness Recovery Action Plan (Copeland, M., 2002), and Appendix Section C-5, Building Mutuality into the Relationship Using WRAP.

Transparency content:

What is WRAP?

WRAP is a self-monitoring system that can help you stay well, feel better, and work on life changes. It includes:

- The Wellness Toolbox
- Daily Maintenance Plan
- Identifying Triggers and an Action Plan
- Identifying Early Warning Signs and an Action Plan
- Signs that Things Are Breaking Down and an Action Plan
- Crisis Planning
- Post Crisis Planning

Why Develop a WRAP (transparency/slide 37)?

WRAP will:

- ☐ Help you stay as well as possible,
- ☐ Help you keep track of difficult feelings and behaviors,
- ☐ Develop action plans to help you feel better, and
- ☐ Tell others what to do for you when you are feeling so badly that it is more difficult to make decisions and take care of yourself.

WRAP can be used as a helpful tool for making life changes like (transparency/slide 38):

- ☐ Getting a job or changing jobs,
- ☐ Taking on more responsibilities,
- ☐ Getting more education or training,
- ☐ Changing your living situation,
- ☐ Moving,
- ☐ Beginning or leaving an intimate relationship, and
- ☐ Working on relationship issues.

WRAP can be used to address other life issues like (transparency/slide 39)

Who develops your WRAP?

There is only one person who can develop your WRAP—YOU (transparency/slide 40). You, and only you, decide:

- ☐ If you want to write one,
- ☐ How much time it takes you to do it,
- ☐ When you want to do it,
- ☐ What you want and don't want in it,

- Which parts you want to do,
- Who you want, if anyone, to help you with it,
- How you use it,
- Who you show it to,
- Where you keep it, and
- Who has copies of your crisis plan.

Two Training Leaders do a 5-minute role-play of working with another person on developing a list of Wellness Tools. Also let the participants know that they could work with their link to develop a WRAP for their Community Links relationship (similar to the WRAP you have developed in the previous sessions).

Reflections on the day

Participants and Training Leaders share what they have learned during the day and what they hope to learn in the next sessions.

Assignment for the next session:

- Ask participants to gather information on resources in their community that might be helpful to a person who is working on community integration. They will bring this information to the next session.
- Review the WRAP process as described in the book, Wellness Recovery Action Plan, and/or in the handout in their manual.

DAY 2

Housekeeping (15 minutes)

Address any questions about the agenda for the day, the facilities and the participant guidelines. Ask each participant to share one thing they did for fun in the last few days. Distribute any handouts developed at the previous session.

Module 1

Sharing Community Resources (20 minutes)

Goal: to share information on resources in the community.

Each participant shares the resources they discovered in their community that might be used by Community Links. These are listed on a sheet of easel-pad paper and developed into a handout for the next meeting.

Thinking About Community (30 minutes)

Goal: to introduce people to the concept of the different kinds of community and working with their Linkee to discover or rediscover their community.

Group members divide into groups with three people in each group (Training Leaders can be included in the groups so the groups are equal). One person in the each group serves as the recorder. People in the group discuss different definitions of community. The recorder records their responses. (10 minutes) The large group reconvenes. One person from each group reports their findings to the larger group. The Training Leader describes the importance of their Linkee defining their own community and the community they would like to feel part of.

Group members share what community means to them in their lives.

Helping in the Community Links Relationship (25 minutes)

Goal: To help participants understand how the Community Links relationship is "peer support," as it is known in the mental health community, and how it differs from traditional mental health services.

Use transparencies/slides 41-44. After reading the first slide to the group, the Training Leader leads the group in a discussion of traditional mental health services. Ask participants to share other ways that traditional mental health services can take away power. Write their comments on a sheet of easel-pad paper to be made into a handout. After reading the second slide, the Training Leader asks the participants to share other ways that people can be encouraged to reclaim their power in Community Links. These are written on a piece of easel-pad paper and developed into a handout.

Transparency content:

Helping in the Community Links Relationship:

Although traditional mental health services are becoming more collaborative, providers sometimes take power away from the person who is receiving services by:

- Diagnosing and labeling people.
- Making predictions about their future.
- Telling people they have a chemical imbalance.
- Ignoring issues related to trauma and abuse.
- Analyzing and judging people's feelings, behaviors and experiences.
- Telling people to avoid taking risks.
- Telling people they will need to take medication for the rest of their lives.

- Taking away hope for recovery and for the future.
- Making decisions about treatment without input from the person involved.
- Keeping chart notes.
- Reporting to other clinicians.
- Avoiding sharing details of their own lives.

In Community Links, people will be encouraged to reclaim their power by:

- Sharing responsibility for the relationship.
- Talking about what hasn't worked in the past and deciding how to do it differently.
- Talking in advance about how to keep the connection strong and handling difficult situations (WRAP for Community Links).
- Looking at things and situations in many different ways.
- Being willing to change ways of thinking, being, and the way you do things.
- Sharing experiences to strengthen connections, create trust, and build hope.
- Considering the effects of trauma and abuse on people's self concept and relationships.
- Supporting and challenging each other to take risks, grow and change.
- Validating people's feelings, behaviors and experiences.

Module 2

Using Language That Promotes Recovery and Community Integration (20 minutes)

Goal: To encourage participants to think about how changing language can affect self-perception, and promote recovery and community integration.

A Training Leader introduces this topic by leading the group in a brief discussion of the power of language. Post two sheets of easel-pad paper side by side. At the top of one sheet write *language that hurts* and at the top of the other sheet write *language that helps.* Ask participants to share common "mental health" words that hurt, words that are filled with negative images and can be used to label someone. The Training Leader can add some key words if they are not brought up by the participants. These might include: high and low functioning, labels of all kinds, chronic, crisis, symptoms, manipulative, acting out, decompensate, and treatment resistant. Then ask them to list, for each word on the list of language that hurts, something that could be said instead that helps. The final list could look like the chart that follows. Use these lists to develop into a handout to be distributed at the next session.

Language that Hurts and Language that Helps:	
Chronic	In recovery
Crisis	Intensity
Symptoms	Experiences/big feelings
"High/low functioning"	"Having a bad/good day"
Manipulative	Strategic
Acting out	Feeling frustrated
"My client"	People I work with
Mentally ill	Feeling different than others
Decompensate	Having a bad day
Noncompliant	Not in agreement with me
Treatment resistant	Considering other options
Safety	Doing something that scares me

Building Trusting and Mutually Supportive Relationships (25 minutes)

Goal: to help participants understand how to build a trusting, mutually supportive relationship with their Linkee.

The Training Leader leads the group in a discussion of why people who are requesting a Community Link find it difficult to trust other people (have been lied to, abused, force treated, taught not to trust our own feelings, perceptions, or thoughts, had our experiences labeled and judged). Write key points on a sheet of easel-pad paper to develop into a handout.

Read transparency/slide 45 to the participants, reminding them that building trust and mutually supportive relationships is often very difficult. Ask people to share from their own experience examples of each point.

Transparency content:

Building Trusting and Mutually Supportive Relationships:

- Having a commitment to share feelings and work through difficult issues,
- Negotiating difficult issues,
- Validating,
- Avoiding categorizing, judging, and evaluation,
- Being honest about what you can and can't do, and about what makes you feel uncomfortable,
- Being respectful with each other,
- Listening closely to what the other person is saying,
- Taking risks with each other,
- Sharing strengths and vulnerabilities,
- Having patience,
- Being there for each other even when the going is rough,
- Asking for help when we need it,
- Being clear about boundaries, and
- Being willing to be uncomfortable.

Ask the group to share other ideas to include in this list. Write their ideas on the easel-pad to be developed into a handout.

A Training Leader leads the group in discussion of the following questions (these questions are in the Participant Manual Appendix, Section C-6):

Building Trusting and Mutually Supportive Relationships

- How do you know when to trust someone? When not to trust?
- What do you think might happen in your relationships with people who have learned not to trust their own thoughts and perceptions? What will you do if you find yourself not trusting/believing what someone else is saying?
- What might you do to help build a sense of trust with someone who clearly doesn't trust you?
- How can you deal with it if someone makes you feel uncomfortable, "pushes your buttons," without having the relationship break down?
- How can you and your link share the power in your relationship? How will you avoid having one person be the helper and the other the person who is helped?
- How will you respond if the person you are working with says something that scares you like, "I am thinking of ending my life"?
- What boundaries will you want to have in your Community Links relationship?

  Examples;

  No phone calls after 9 at night,

  Only one phone call a day,

  Not meeting in each other's homes,

  No loaning or borrowing,

  No asking for money, and

  No going in bars.

Negotiating the Relationship (20 minutes)

Goal: To give participants practice in negotiating difficult issues and circumstances.

The Training Leader reads each of the following scenarios to the group and asks them to share how this situation can be handled in a way that promotes mutual responsibility. What might you do in each of the following scenarios to get back to mutual responsibility? (These scenarios are in the Appendix C-7.)

Negotiating the Relationship Scenarios

1. You're in a coffee shop with the person you are supporting. He/she starts getting really loud and you're afraid you might get thrown out of the restaurant.
2. The person you're working with tells you that you have no idea what you're doing and that he/she would rather be in the hospital where "people are professionals."
3. The person you're working with says that they're feeling like this is just too hard and maybe they'd rather just end it.
4. The person you're working with says something that really offends you (for example, makes a racial slur…)
5. Every time you show up to do something with the other person, they've been drinking. Alcohol is prohibited on their court order.
6. You've noticed that the person you're working with smells pretty bad most of the time and people in town make faces or walk way around you when you're in town.

Module 3

Listing Skills (45 minutes)

Goal: To help participants develop listening skills that will enhance their Community Links relationship.

Ask participants to share stories of times when:

- Someone really listened to them and seemed interested, curious, and non-judgmental, and how that felt.
- Someone validated their feelings and they had a sense that the other person really understood, and how that felt (for example, “that sounds really hard”).
- Someone reflected their feelings so that they knew the other person understood how they felt, and how that felt for you (like, “that must make you feel really sad”)
- Someone made sure they understood what you were saying by reflecting back what you said, and how that felt.
- Someone spoke to you using language you didn’t understand and what that felt like.

Ask participants to share things they could say to a person to get more clarity on what they are saying or encourage them to share more. “Help me understand?” “I wonder.” “How did you learn…?” “What makes that so…?” “How would you like it to turn out?” “What can we do to get there?”

Ask participants to share questions that focus on what people want in their lives, questions that give them a sense of their power. “What do you want?” “Do your current beliefs support what you want?” “What would you have to believe to have what you want?” “What do you want to feel?” “If you were feeling that way, what would you be able to do?”

Listening Practice (30 minutes)

Goal: To help participants understand the importance of listening.

The Training Leader tells the participants that, in their Community Links relationship, it will be vital to listen closely to what the other person is saying, and to avoid interrupting with stories of their own, advice, and judgments. Participants share brief stories of times when another person listened closely to them and how it was helpful.

Participants divide into pairs. Each person gets 5 minutes to talk to the other person about anything they choose to share. They can rant, rave, get angry—whatever feels right to them. The Training Leaders keep track of the time and advises people when it is time to change from listener to talker. If necessary a Training Leader can take part in this activity so everyone gets a chance to share and to listen. Participants regroup and share how the listening felt to them.

Module 4

First Contact (35 minutes)

Goal: To help the participants have an effective first meeting with their Linkee.

Tell the participants that their first meeting with their Linkee will be a three-way meeting that includes the Community Link and the Program Coordinator. At this meeting, the three of you will discuss what the Community Links program is, things the two of you might like to do together, concerns any of you have, and arrange the next meeting.

The Training Leader will read the points on transparencies/slides 46 and 47) about the first meeting the two of you will have, here referred to as "first contact".

Transparency content:

First Contact

Be aware that you may both be nervous or uneasy, even though you have met before. Get together in a place that is comfortable for both of you, a place you arranged in your meeting with the Program Coordinator.

You can discuss:

- What each of you knows about Community Links;
- Times when connections with others have helped you get back on your feet;
- Times when you perceived yourself one way, as a mental patient or as an incompetent person, changed that view to a positive one, and how that changed your life;
- Strengths—you may need to point out the person's strengths, like courage and persistence;
- How the relationship can be mutually beneficial; and
- Things the two of you could do together.

Focus your discussion on life and living, and away from a focus on symptoms and mental illness.

Avoid statements or questions like (transparency/slide 48):

- I am going to help you recover from your mental illness.
- I am Bill. I have had schizophrenia for years.
- I am Sally. I don't have a mental illness. Tell me what it is like for you to have a mental illness. Did other people in your family have a mental illness? How long have you had a mental illness?

Talking about First Contact

People break into pairs and practice first contact for 5 minutes each (each participant taking a turn at being the Community Link and the Linkee).

Reconvene as a large group to discuss this experience.

Advocacy, Rights and Responsibilities (35 minutes)

Goal: To help participants understand, and be able to work with their Linkee on self-advocacy, rights, and responsibilities

A Training leader reads transparency/slide 49 to group members. Before the session, the Training Leader needs to read the handout on self-advocacy (Appendix C-8) and the Personal Bill of Rights (Appendix C-9) so she or he can add detail to each step. Tell participants about this handout that is also included in the Participant Manual that describes each of the following steps in detail. Participants can use this as a guide when they are working with their Linkee on self-advocacy.

Transparency content:

Steps in Self-Advocacy

1. Believe in yourself,
2. Know your rights,
3. Decide what you want or what you are working toward,
4. Get the facts,
5. Plan your strategy,
6. Gather your support,
7. Target your efforts,

8. Express yourself clearly,
9. Assert yourself calmly, and
10. Be firm and persistent.

Hang two sheets of easel-pad paper side by side on the wall. Label one sheet *rights in the community.* Label the other sheet *responsibilities in the community.* Ask participants to share their rights in the community (to be treated with dignity, compassion and respect, and to use community services like the library, post office, and recreation facilities). Then ask them to list responsibilities in the community (treating others with dignity and respect, not interfering with the rights of others to use community facilities).

Participants volunteer to do brief role modeling of supporting people in having their rights respected, such as using public transportation, attending community events, and accessing needed services. They also role model taking responsibility in the community, such as being respectful in the library, following smoking regulations, volunteering to clean at community events.

Closing

Reflections on the day.

Assignment: Ask participants to do a deeper study of their community to discover even more resources that might be available to people.

Day 3

Housekeeping (15 minutes)

Address any questions about the agenda for the day, the facilities and the participant guidelines. Ask each participant to share one thing they did for fun in the last few days. Distribute any handouts developed at the previous session.

Module 1

Getting Together (55 minutes)

Goal: To give participants an opportunity to practice first contact and develop an activity schedule with another person.

A Training Leader reads transparencies/slides 50 and 51 to the group, solicits further ideas from the group, and asks for questions. Allow 45 minutes for the second part of this activity. The participants can refer to Appendix C-10 (Getting Together), 11 (Capacity Inventory-Ideas for Focus), and 12 (the Community Links Scheduling Form).

Transparency content:

Getting Together

1. The Community Link and the person they link with can use their time together in any way that is agreeable to both of them.
2. If the person is in a treatment facility, arrange to meet them there. When the person has left the facility, meet at a place that is agreeable to both people.
3. At the first session, develop plans for the first few times you will get together. You could also plan for the next meeting only.

4. Getting together for two hours, once or twice a week, at the convenience of both people is suggested. It can be more or less, depending on what is possible and needed for the Community Links.
5. Meetings can be a mix of social time and time working on issues and activities related to community integration.
6. Be flexible about what will happen at a session. Change plans to best meet needs.

Participants divide into groups of three. The Training Leaders participate to make the groups even. People take turns playing the role of the Community Link, the Linkee, and being an observer. They role play for 10 minutes, getting together with the Linkee for the first time and beginning to develop plans for their time together. They then spend 5 minutes asking for feedback from the observer and discussing the role play.

Gradually Reducing the Community Link Relationship (20 minutes)

Goal: To help Community Links understand how to gradually step back as the Linkee develops natural supports and becomes more connected to the community.

Participants share indicators that they can gradually reduce their involvement with the other person. These are written on a sheet of easel-pad paper and made into a handout for the next session. Ideas could include when the person is:

- Attending a support group on their own,
- Reaching out to others more often for assistance and support,
- Feeling more comfortable in the community,
- More willing to self-advocate,
- Venturing into the community alone, and/or

- [ ] Has several new friends.

Module 2

Community Links Values (25 minutes)

Goal: To familiarize participants with the values of the Community Links program, and to monitor their own adherence to these values.

The Training Leader reviews the values listed on transparencies/slides 52-54. Discuss the values as needed. Ask participants to share other values they think should be included in Community Links. Participants share ways they can monitor themselves to be sure they are adhering to these values. List these indicators on the easel pad and make them into a handout.

Transparency content:

Community Links Values

1. Community Links help people to understand that they can take back control of their lives, become independent, have natural supports—that they can do the things they want to do with their lives, and that there is no limit to what they can achieve.
2. Community Links supports self-determination, personal responsibility, empowerment and self-advocacy.
3. Community Links is a reciprocal relationship in which people treat each other as equals with dignity, compassion, respect, and unconditional high regard.
4. In Community Links there is acceptance of each person as she or he is—unique, special individuals, including acceptance of diversity with relation to cultural, ethnic, religious, racial, gender, age, disability and sexual preference issues.
5. Community Links is a totally voluntary program.

6. In Community Links, each person is recognized as the expert on her or himself.
7. Community Links use common language rather than clinical, medical and diagnostic language.
8. Community Links work together to increase mutual understanding, knowledge and promote wellness.
9. Community Links validate each other's experiences, including experiences of trauma and abuse.
10. Community Links focus on strengths and away from perceived deficits.
11. Community Links are responsible for their own behavior and do not use symptoms as an excuse for bad behavior.
12. Community Links use honest, direct, and respectful communication.
13. Community Links share power and responsibility.
14. Community Links relationships are confidential.
15. Community Links enjoy being and working together.

Values in Action (30 minutes)

Goal: To give Community Links practice in monitoring their adherence to program values.

A Training Leader reads each of the following scenarios to the group. Group members also have a copy of these scenarios in their manual. The group discusses the situation, deciding the values that are being demonstrated or ignored. These scenarios are in Appendix Section C-13. Participants may want to make notes on their description.

Values in Action Scenarios

1. You've been working on a WRAP plan with the person you're linked with. It has been going very well until this week when the person tells you he/she thinks this is a waste of time and that he/she doesn't want to work on it anymore. You say, "But you're so close…if we just finish this today, you'll see how much better it will make you feel."
2. The person you're working with seems more tired and uninterested than usual. You ask if he/she has been taking his/her medications.
3. When you go to pick up the person you're working with, one of the group home staff ask you how the person seems to be doing. You say, "Thanks for asking, I'll go get (name of person) and maybe he/she can share with us what he/she thinks about Community Links."
4. The person you're working with does something that makes you really uncomfortable but you're afraid you'll hurt his/her feelings if you say something. You act like nothing is wrong but then go back to the Program Coordinator and say that you no longer want to work with this person.
5. The person you're working with has really been enjoying your company. He/she wants to spend more time with you. Your response is that the hours set up for Community Links are nonnegotiable.

Ask participants to share which values they think will be hardest for them to follow and why that would be so. Work together as a group to resolve these issues.

How Do We Know Community Links Is Working? (20 minutes)

Goal: To help people understand how they can assess their participation in Community Links.

A Training Leader asks participants to share instances where something wasn't working for them but they were afraid to speak honestly about it, describe how it worked out, and how in retrospect, they could deal with it differently another time.

The Training Leader explains that in Community Links, you will work together to evaluate the success of what you're doing. That means you will want and need to be honest and respectful. This can be a challenge. If this is an expectation right from the beginning, and you're honest and respectful, it will become a natural part of what you do.

Both people in the Community Links relationship work together to answer the following questions (transparencies/slides 55 and 56). Do it often, perhaps every other week. They will guide you in thinking about and recognizing how this program is working for both of you, and help you plan future activities and make changes in the way you want to do things.

Transparency content:

Community Links Evaluation Questions

1. How is this relationship working for you? What do you like about it? What would you like to change? How could we make that change in a way that would work well for both of us?
2. Are you sharing honestly how you feel in Community? If not, why not? How can we make it possible for you to share what you feel in this relationship? Are you asking for what you want and need? If not, why not? How can we make that possible?

3. What has changed about the way you think about things since the beginning of Community Links?
4. What do we need to do more of or less of to make sure that Community Links is working for both of us?
5. After you have done this with the person you are working with, both of you can discuss these same questions with the person responsible for program evaluation.

To practice sharing honestly and respectfully, ask group members to answer the following questions.

- How has this training worked for you? What have you liked about it? What would you change about this training?
- Did you share honestly how you felt in this training. If so, what made it possible for you to do so? If not, why not?
- Did you ask for what you need and want? If so, what made it possible for you to do so? If not, why not?
- How has your thinking changed in this training?

Module 3

Report on Community Resources (15 minutes)

Goal: To expand people's understanding of the resources that are available in the community that might be helpful to the person they are working with.

Participants share the resources they have discovered in their communities. These are recorded on an easel-pad and made into a handout that people can include in their binder. Training leaders describe and demonstrate how participants can develop resource binders with the person they are working with in the Community Links program. Members of the group share problems they anticipate where people have difficulty accessing and using these community resources. Each problem is written across the top of a sheet of easel pad paper. Participants and Training Leaders share possible solutions. These are recorded on the easel pad and developed into handouts to include in their Community Links binder.

Community Links Protocols (60 minutes)

Goal: To advise participants about program protocols, and to assure that people leave the training with the information they need to participate in the program.

Training leaders advise participants about program specifics including:

Stipends or payment (when they will be paid, how they will be paid, how much they will be paid). This will vary from program to program. Some programs may not be able to provide any payment and others may be able to compensate people.

Reimbursement for travel and expenses. Sponsoring programs need to have funds available to reimburse people for travel expenses, and, if they can, costs like movie and concert tickets and memberships.

Liability coverage. Sponsoring organizations will have liability coverage for people who are part of their organization. This will include Community Links. People involved in the program may need to fill out forms to assure that they receive this coverage.

Timelines for matching people with their link. Some programs will have people already requesting links before the training. Others may do the recruiting after the training. Let people know when they can expect this to happen and arrange meeting dates if possible.

Specifics of the initial meeting with their Linkee and the Program Coordinator. Before people start working together, they will meet with the Program Coordinator to be introduced and to discuss the program.

Reporting and evaluation. Community links can advise the Program Coordinator about how often they are meeting and general information about the kinds of things they are doing together. The Community Links can set up a schedule of meetings at least once a month, either by phone or in person, to evaluate their work in the program, addressing the questions in the handout in Appendix C-14. All personal information needs to remain confidential.

Stories. Collecting stories about Community Links is a powerful way of documenting the program. Encourage all participants to write stories, and, if they feel comfortable doing so, sharing the stories with the Program Coordinator and possibly including them in a program report. These stories provide evidence of the value of the program.

Pass out any forms such as travel reimbursement forms and liability insurance forms.

Questions. Allow plenty of time for questions.

Module 4

Problem Solving

Participants share problems they anticipate in being a Community Link. Each problem is written across the top of a piece of easel-pad paper. Group members and Training Leaders share responses. These are written on the easel-pad. That sheet is given to the person who shared the problem.

Closing

Participants and Training Leaders share their thoughts and feelings about the training. Each participant is given a Community Links Certificate (Appendix D).

Note about Certificates: The Certificates can be made on certificate paper that can be purchased at a stationary store. The blank certificate can be copied on the certificate paper, filling in the person's name, the date and having it signed by the Training Leaders. The certificates can also be made on a computer by putting certificate paper in the printer and printing each participant name individually along with the date on the certificate. The Training Leaders sign the certificates.

Appendix

Appendix A

Readings for Training Leader

A-1.

Crisis as an Opportunity for Growth and Change

by Shery Mead

The concept of crisis in mental health is an interesting one. In spite of the fact that many traditional theorists have viewed crisis as an opportunity for growth and as an essential experience in the context of one's development (Erikson, 1976), we in mental health want to medicate it, lock it up, and restrain it. We have forgotten that perhaps there is something we can learn from this experience, something that will enable us to "do" it differently and understand ourselves in new ways.

Many of us, at times have felt out of control, that our pain was more than we could manage and even that life was not worth living. It has left us feeling isolated, alone, different and "crazy." It is not something that most of us want to go through again and again. And yet, we have been told and have come to believe that it is something that "happens" to us because of our illness. We are told that we are "decompensating" and that the goal is to return to a "premorbid" state. And so we go through life afraid of when it will happen next, believing that we must be careful not to get "stressed," believing that we are fragile and out of control without our medications and our services. Instead of living life we learn to avoid it as if it were dangerous. We have come to believe this because our experiences have been named for us. We are no longer individuals with unique perspectives, but rather a set of generic symptoms that need a generic treatment. Though being labeled has been helpful to some, others of us have found it debilitating and limiting.

Peer support can offer a fundamentally different approach to crisis in that there are fewer assumptions about what it is people are experiencing. People may compare stories and strategies and ways of making meaning, but in the end, no one person has the power to name or to treat. The following is a way of thinking about being with people even through very difficult time—a way that that honors crisis as an opportunity to learn and grow and, most importantly, stay connected.

1. Building mutual relationships. It is only in relationships that are constantly negotiated that we build mutual respect and trust. When we consider that both of us have needs and expertise, we learn from each other while taking chances in becoming more vulnerable and consequently more whole. As we take new risks in relationship, we find ourselves breaking out of old roles and assumptions, opening doors to self and relational discoveries that we never before knew existed.
2. Being with "big" feelings. We are not a culture that has a lot of tolerance for intensity or "big" feelings. We tend to want to calm people down or make it stop because we are uncomfortable. In peer support we can recognize that people have a lot of big feelings and they aren't all dangerous. They are in fact, rich with information.
3. Understanding the "story." I've always thought it was interesting that when people were having tough times they were always asked what was wrong with them. What if, for example we asked, "What happened to you?" Could we begin to understand the ways that people's versions of their own stories impact the way they make meaning of their experiences now?

4. Sharing ways that "stories" are understood. One of the most valuable aspects of peer support is our ability to share our stories with each other. It's amazing to me what happens the first time we realize that we're not the only person who's been through some of these things. We can hear how each of us has learned to think about ourselves and can share strategies that take our whole story into account.
5. Challenging the current story. When trusting relationships develop and when both people are in control of the relationship, we can gently begin to challenge the ways each of us have learned to make meaning of our experiences. We can let each other know what works for us and what doesn't. Perhaps we are not decompensating. Maybe we're justifiably angry and we don't know ways to express it. Perhaps we're not in suicidal depression; maybe we just feel tremendous shame and guilt for things we learned to believe were "our fault." When people compare and share, inevitably new stories are created and relationships deepen.
6. Creating a new, shared story. As relationships deepen we tend to take more risks, share our vulnerabilities and try on ways of "seeing" that were not previously available to us. We find ourselves in the process of examining our own beliefs and assumptions and we continuously try these out in relationship. We find that we are growing through the context of relationship. There are no limits to the possibilities because there are no static roles. We have the opportunity to be vulnerable and strong, helper and helped. We find that others are finding hope through our successes and that they are taking new risks.

Peer support is a culture of healing. As people practice new ways of "being" through even the most difficult times, possibilities for breaking old patterns and creating new opportunities are endless. Crisis then just becomes another word for redefining our experience and ourselves and instead of needing to be locked up, we can begin to break free.

A-2.

Peer Support: A Definition

by Shery Mead

Peer support is a system of giving and receiving help founded on key principles of respect, shared responsibility, and mutual agreement of what is helpful. Peer support is not based on psychiatric models and diagnostic criteria. It is about understanding another's situation empathically through the shared experience of emotional and psychological pain. When people find affiliation with others whom they feel are like them, they feel a connection. This connection, or affiliation, is a deep, holistic understanding based on mutual experience where people are able to be with each other without the constraints of traditional (expert/patient) relationships. Further, as trust in the relationship builds, both people are able to respectfully challenge each other when they find themselves reenacting old roles. This allows members of the peer community to try out new behaviors with one another and move beyond previously held self-concepts built on disability, diagnosis, and trauma worldview. The Stone Center refers to this as mutual empowerment (Stiver & Miller, 1998 *The Healing Connection.* Boston, MA).

Peer support starts with the basic assumption that meaning and perception are created within the context of culture and relationships. Our self-definition, how we understand and interpret our experiences and how we relate to others is created and developed from the direct and indirect messages we get from others and the messages we get from dominant cultural beliefs and assumptions. We find that many of us who have used mental health services have been told what we "have," how "it" will be treated and how we must think about arranging our lives around this "thing." We have then begun to see our lives as a series of problems or "symptoms" and we have forgotten that there might be other ways to interpret our experiences.

Because of this we have felt different and alone and "other-than" much of our lives, leaving us in relationships that have been less than mutually empowering and more often than not, destructive and infantilizing. We have learned to understand our experiences as signs of illness while burying histories of past violence and abuse. We have lost our power and our choices in most relationships. We have learned to either "act as if," or we have become dependent on professional interpretation of our everyday experiences. It is not uncommon for us to then offer (and ask for) help based on this model.

Peer support training can help develop our ability to think critically about who we've become. Training helps us learn to sit with discomfort while we explore the relational dynamics that have kept us stuck, and also helps us look at our own reactivity. It is helpful to understand people's "hot spots," and the kinds of situations that feel comfortable, tolerable, or absolutely intolerable so we can learn to negotiate power rather than take it. This then allows us to normalize what has been named as abnormal because of other people's discomfort. Discovering this in a peer community reveals a different way of understanding our behaviors and presents an excellent framework to explore personal and relational change.

One of the more significant (and dramatic) practices has been the development of peer-run crisis respite programs. Theses programs emerged as an alternative to traditional psychiatric hospitalization and have been at the cutting edge of developing new practices for responding to crisis. They are essentially grounded in the knowledge that crisis can be transforming, that mutually supportive relationships provide necessary connection, and that new contexts offer new ways of thinking about one's experience. Rather than objectifying and naming the crisis experience in relation to the construct of illness (e.g. "You're getting sick again") people proactively and dialogically create a plan that serves as a guideline and reminder as to what kinds of interactions and activities will support a positive outcome for everyone. Out of this shared dynamic a sense of trust is built and the crisis can emerge as an opportunity to create new meaning around the experience while offering people mutually respectful relationships. As trust builds in the relationships and people feel valued, new ways of thinking, doing, and living become possible. The situation is shared rather than "handled," and it offers an opportunity for tremendous community growth.

Peer support programs must also challenge the current system's approach to how people with histories of abuse are treated. The devastating impact of abuse must be recognized for what it is and not viewed as psychiatric pathology or biologic brain disorders. Through peer support services we can offer each other relationships that are respectful of our experiences, our ways of communicating, and how we have learned to tell our story. We can challenge each other to both face and to move beyond these stories and patterns. We can build new community norms that replace the illness environments that have kept us trapped. Finally, we can conscientiously name and expose the cultural violence that caused us to end up in these institutions. If we can learn to tell our stories in new ways, we can create communities where the sanctioned outcomes include noncompliance to "mental patient" identities or expectations, rejection of unhelpful treatment regimens, the questioning of overuse of medication, and speaking out about the prevalence of trauma and abuse. Finally, we can to call into question whose problem it really is.

It is no small feat for peer programs to develop this level of critical self-awareness. We are asking people to act in ways that are not instinctual and we are operating on a level of discomfort that shakes our very realities. It is here however, in community, that narrative becomes transformed. This means an entirely new interpretive framework for our construction of crisis/problem and our construction of help. In other words, we begin to understand change and learning not as an individual process, but rather one where we continuously construct knowledge from actions and reactions, conversations and the ongoing building of consensus. Rather than thinking about personal symptom reduction we are talking about real social change.

A-3.

Healing and Social Action

by Shery Mead

Those of us with histories of past trauma often feel "other-than." We have been told again and again that something is wrong with us, that we're "crazy," that it was our fault, and that we're bad. We have learned that our very lives are dependent on not trusting ourselves. We learn that what we know, based on what we see, feel, and experience is not "true." What has become our truth—what is our reality—has been defined or named by others, not by us. Our instinctive feelings of terror, anger, and despair have never been accepted or acceptable and so our feelings and perceptions become linked to the "truth" that we have embodied.

It is with these beliefs that we have sought mental health treatment for "our problems." If we have been lucky (and economically privileged) we may have found treatment that supports us in finding and rebuilding our voice, and helps us to move away from seeing ourselves as the problem. If we've not been so lucky, our actions (or others' assessment of our actions) may have led us to further abuse in terms of forced treatment, locked doors, physical restraints, and debilitating medications. Either way, we have been labeled with a psychiatric diagnosis and our experience has become further embedded in the "self as problem," and our pain as a symptom to be treated. We again have learned to view ourselves and our experiences through others' eyes, and we learn to believe that we are "mentally ill."

Peer support can offer a fundamentally different framework for understanding our experiences and perceptions of our past, present, and future. It can provide us with opportunities to find new ways of understanding our world and our experiences and of finding new ways to respond to it. In peer support we can learn to form relationships outside of the definition or context of "illness" and to talk about the effects of trauma and abuse in our lives. We can share our stories with each other and we can begin to question how and why other people have learned to tell their stories in the ways that they do. We can begin to listen to each other in new ways, hearing the story rather than evaluating and assessing the problem. We can be witnesses to each other's pain. And most importantly we can validate the reality of each other's feelings, perceptions, and experiences. These conversations can influence the ways that we respond to the situations we face, the ways we think about things, and can ultimately lead to our healing.

As we challenge the naming of our experience by others we shake the whole foundation of a trauma worldview, and we begin to identify the larger cultural context in which we have been situated. As we unite in shared experiences and begin to expose the very structures that have kept us silenced, we find that "doing" social action becomes inextricably linked to healing—personally, relationally and culturally. It is through this collective healing that real change happens, healing in fact that may prevent the creation of future mental patients.

Appendix B

Program information and forms

B-1.

Outline of Promotional Presentation

The following outline could be used to give a presentation to a group of people who are interested in becoming a Community Link, and/or people who would like a Community Link. Think about what you are going to say ahead of time but try to avoid reading what you want to share.

1. Introduce yourself. Share your name, where you live and a few facts about yourself such as, "I am the mother of three small children. Now that the children are in school, I have some time to assist with the Community Links." You might want to explain why you feel the Community Links Program is important and, without breaking confidentiality, share a story or stories of people who have benefited from the program (about 8 minutes).
2. Describe the Community Links Program. Get ideas on what you want to present from the Community Links description at the beginning of the Community Links Manual and from the training session, Day 1—Module 2. You could make a poster or transparencies to emphasize the key point you want to make and to help guide yourself through the presentation. Or use the transparencies from the training, Day 1—Module 2, reading them to the attendees (about 20 minutes).

3. Become involved. Explain how people can become involved in Community Links by either being a Community Link or working with a Community Link. Have contact information and application forms available.
4. Ask for questions from the group. Encourage a lively discussion.
5. Be available after the meeting so people can ask you additional questions.

B-2. Promotional Poster

Tired of waiting for good things

to happen in your life?

Community Links:

Pathways to Reconnection and Recovery

Community Links is a free, voluntary program that connects people who want to regain their independence, make friends, rebuild community connections, work on their own recovery and wellness, and take back control of their own life.

You might like a Community Link!

Call this confidential number, 1-800_____________toll free to learn more about this voluntary, confidential, free program.

B-3.

Application to Be a Community Link

If you would like to provide this information by phone, please call ....

Name ____

Address ____

Phone Number ________________________ Email ________________

I want to be a Community Link with a person who is working on mental health recovery and improving the quality of their life, independence and increased involvement with the community because:

I have the following qualifications for being a Community Link:

I have the following experience that would make me an effective Community Link:

___ I am willing to attend a three-day training and to devote several hours a week to this program.

You can contact the following people as references:

Name ____

Address ______________________________________

Phone number ________________

Name ____

Address ______________________________________

Phone number ________________

Name ____

Address ______________________________________

Phone number ________________

Mail or fax the application to:

You can deliver the application to:

The application needs to be in the office by: (date)

B-4.

Community Links Participant Form

You can supply this information by phone or by meeting with the Community Links by calling

1-800-_____________ Send this application or take it to (Community Links address)

Fax it to (Community Links fax number Email it to (Community Links email address)

Name ____________________ Date ______________________

Address ____

Phone number __________________ E-mail ___________________

What do you hope to get out of the Community Links Program?

Do you have people in your life now that you consider your "community"? Is so, please describe that "community."

What would you like your community to be like?

What would it be like for you if you felt like you were integrated into your community?

What kinds of things are you interested in?

What kinds of things do you like to do?

What places do you like to go?

Are you an active or more sedentary person?

Do you like to exercise? If so, what kinds of exercise do you prefer?

Do you like to talk a lot or do you tend to be quiet? Are you a good listener?

What kinds of experiences have you had in the community—both good and bad?

What kind of activities in your community would you like to be involved in?

What kinds of places would you like to go and feel comfortable?

Do you have an easy or difficult time making and keeping friends? If you have a difficult time making and keeping friends, why do you think that is?

Do you like to have lots of friends or do you prefer to have a few friends?

Do you like to attend gatherings where there are lots of people, like concerts, or do you prefer smaller gatherings or just getting together with one other person?

Are you interested in learning about managing mental health difficulties and hard times in your life?

Other information that may be helpful in matching with a Community Link

Appendix C

To be copied for Community Links Training Participant Binder

C-1.

Community Links Agenda Overview

Day 1

8:45–9:00 Housekeeping

9:00–10:30 Module 1

- □ Introductions
- □ Participant guidelines
- □ Defining the issue

10:30–10:45 Break

10:45 12:15 Module 2

- □ Describing Community Links and the role of Community Links

12:15–1:00 Lunch

1:00–2:30 Module 3

- □ Developing a Community Links Wellness Recovery Action Plan

2:30–2:45 Break

2:45–4:15 Module 4

- □ Developing a Community Links Wellness Recovery Action Plan (continued)
- □ Description of personal WRAP process and how to use it in Community Links

4:15–4:30

- □ Reflections on the day and assignment for the next session

Day 2

8:45–9:00 Housekeeping

9:15–10:30 Module 1

- Sharing community resources
- Thinking about community
- Helping in the Community Links relationship

10:30–10:45 Break

10:45–12:15 Module 2

- Using language that promotes recovery and community integration
- Building trusting and mutually supportive relationships
- Negotiating the relationship

12:15–1:00 Lunch

1:00–2:30 Module 3

- Listening skills
- Listening practice

2:30–2:45 Break

2:45–4:15 Module 4

- First Contact
- Advocacy, rights and responsibilities

4:15–4:30

- Reflections on the day

Assignment—Returning to the community to discover more resources.

Day 3

8:45–9:00 Housekeeping

9:00–10:30 Module 1

- Getting together
- Gradually reducing the Community Link relationship

10:30–10:45 Break

10:45–12:15 Module 2

- Community Links values
- Values in action
- How do we know Community Links is working

12:15–1:00 Lunch

1:00–2:30 Module 3

- Report on community resources
- Community Links protocols

2:30–2:45 Break

2:45–4:00 Module 4

- Group problem solving

4:00–4:30

- Reflections on the training and celebration

C-2. Community Links PowerPoint Presentation Thumbnail Sketches

Community Links:

Pathways to Reconnection and Recovery

Defining the Issue

While many people who have experienced mental health difficulties are recovering and moving on with their lives, there are many people who:

- have lost hope and their ability to self advocate
- have stopped working toward meeting their life goals and dreams
- are treated badly and/or stigmatized by others
- have become separated and ostracized from their natural supports and their community

2

- seem stuck in the mental health system
- are dependent on the mental health system for most or all aspects of their daily lives
- may have had repeated commitment orders or a court order that limits their freedom and may include involuntary hospitalization and forced treatment
- may live in a group home, supported housing or community care facility or an institution
- don't have a home

3

What do people in this circumstance want?

The Moving Ahead study showed that people want:

- to be treated well
- to feel accepted in their families
- to have friends and supporters outside of the mental health system
- to be a part of their community

1

- to learn to use mental health recovery skills and strategies
- to have recovery security so they can recover without fear of losing benefits and services
- be able to do the things they like to do
- to work toward their own goals and dreams

5

The Community Link and the person they are working with:

- Connect and build reciprocal relationships where they can learn and grow together
- Model the kinds of relationships that people would have in the community
- Learn their strengths and use these strengths to link with activities and people in the community
- Talk openly about what each of them needs in the relationship like honesty, mutuality and respect

6

- Accept each other as they are
- Focus on strengths, possibilities and successes
- Are clear about expectations like being on time, being in contact if appointments can't be kept, and respecting agreed upon boundaries
- Discuss and respect each person's boundaries
- Keep personal information confidential

7

- Share difficult times they have had, along with details of how they resolved the situations
- Decide how to handle difficult situations that may arise
- Set up a schedule of things they can do together (or decide after each visit what they will do the next time)
- Discover resources in the community that might be fun, interesting or helpful
- Work on developing a system of natural supports

8

- Attend meetings, groups and workshops together
- Work on developing personal Wellness Recovery Action Plans or a Wellness Recovery Action Plan for their relationship
- Evaluate their relationship
- Assist with overall program monitoring and evaluation
- Work gradually toward a time when the Community Link is no longer needed in that role, and the person has natural supports and feels comfortable in the community

9

What Community Links do:

- **LISTEN**
- Assists and support the other person in making personal decisions
- Offer ideas and suggestions
- Point out the other person's strengths

10

- Remind the other person that there is no limit to what they can do
- Remind the other person that they have the right to work toward their own goals and dreams
- Share simple, safe things a person can do to feel well and to get through difficult times
- Work with the other person on developing a personal Wellness Recovery Action Plan

11

- Assist the person in developing a circle of natural supports and feeling comfortable in the community
- Treat the other person in ways that make her or him feel respected
- Reach out for assistance and support from the Program Coordinator
- Work toward a time when the person no longer needs the Community Links relationship (they may still be friends and even mutual supporters)

12

Community Links don't:

- Try to be, or act like, experts
- Tell the other person what to do
- Judge, evaluate or try to analyze the other person
- Focus on problems and illness
- Make assumptions about the other person

13

- Violate the other person's boundaries
- Loan the other person money or things
- Get into an intimate or sexual relationship with each other
- Meet in bars
- Use coercion or threats

14

- Do anything that violates a court order
- Talk about each other behind the other person's back
- Report specifics of their Community Links relationship to any agency, care provider, family member or other supporter

15

"If Community Links works for you, what will be different in your life?"

- Goal: To help people think more deeply about what participation in this program will mean to them.
- Each participant is asked to share what they think will be different in their life if this program works for them. Responses are recorded and given as a handout.

16

Wellness Recovery Action Plan

- Wellness Toolbox
- Daily Maintenance Plan
  What I'm like when I feel well
  What I need to do every day to feel well
  Things I might need to do to feel well
- Triggers and a Triggers Action Plan
- Early Warning Signs and an Early Warning Signs Action Plan
- When Things are Breaking Down and an Action Plan
- Crisis Plan
- Post Crisis Plan

17

Community Links Wellness Toolbox

- Validating the other person's experiences
- Being honest with each other
- Open discussion of an issue
- Doing something fun together
- Doing something different
- Doing something together that neither of you have ever done

18

- Doing something together that neither of you have ever done
- Peer counseling
- Giving the other person listening time
- Discussing a topic of mutual concern
- Staying present in the situation
- Taking a break from the relationship

19

- Making a schedule
- Revising the schedule
- Spending more time together
- Spending less time together
- Arranging calls between the times you get together
- Searching for new community resources
- Going to an event in the community together

20

- Attending a support group together
- Attending a meeting of a special interest group
- Checking out the newspaper Community Calendar listings

21

Community Links Relationship is Going Well

- Both participants feel satisfied with the relationship
- The participants feel comfortable being together
- Participants look forward to spending time together
- People can take risks together

22

- People challenge each other
- Neither person has more power than the other person
- There is easy conversation
- The relationship is fun

23

Things to do each time you get together

- Have a comfortable place to meet
- Arrive on time
- Spend a few minutes at the beginning of the time together talking about things that have happened recently and getting reacquainted
- Decide if what you had planned to do is what you really need and want to do
- Review and respond to the evaluation questions
- Make a plan for the next time you will get together.

24

Things you can do when you get together

- Peer counsel
- Have a conversation
- Listen
- Make a list of Wellness Tools
- Work on a Wellness Recovery Action Plan
- Go to a restaurant for a cup of coffee
- Talk about work possibilities
- Visit a possible job site
- Go to the local senior center
- Attend a support group
- Go to an exercise class

25

- Go to a movie or a concert
- Go to the library
- Shop
- Organize
- Get together with several other people
- Make a list of places in the community you would like to visit together
- Pay bills
- Make appointments

26

Things that could happen in your lives or the community that might affect the Community Links relationship

- A time together is missed because of bad weather
- A person is having difficulty with benefits
- You visit a place together and are treated badly
- The two of you have a misunderstanding
- One of you forgets an appointment you had with each other

27

- You can't do something you had planned because your car breaks down
- One of you has a tragedy in your family
- One of you has an accident or a serious illness
- A horrible thing happens in your community
- A horrible thing happens in the world

28

Community Links Wellness Tools
to get through difficult times

- Talk on the phone
- Spend lots of time talking
- Do peer counseling
- Spend extra time together
- Arrange to meet at another time
- Review your wellness tools and choose to do several of them
- Discuss the situation with the program coordinator
- Give yourselves a treat
- Cook some food or a meal for the other person

29

Early warning signs that the relationship isn't going well

- The person keeps canceling time that you agreed to spend together
- It's hard to find things to say to each other
- The two of you can't think of anything you'd like to do together
- It feels like a chore to get together

30

- The relationship feels uncomfortable to one or both of you
- One or both of you are beginning to think of ending the relationship
- After you leave your time together you feel badly

31

Tools you could use if you notice early warning signs

- Change your plans
- Get together less often or more often
- Go to a movie or a concert
- Watch a video together
- Peer counseling
- Make some food together and eat it
- Change your plans
- Discuss the situation with the program coordinator

32

The Community Links relationship is going badly

- One of you wants to end the relationship
- There is a lack of trust.
- One of you is having mental health difficulties
- One of you is in the hospital
- One of you is overmedicated and is sleeping during your time together
- You are being rude to each other

33

Tools you could use to improve or save the relationship if things are going badly

- Spend time listening to the other person without giving advice or judging
- Discuss the situation openly
- Peer counsel
- Ask the person what you can do to help

34

- Ask them what has happened
- Ask the other person what needs to change and see if that change is possible
- Talk to the program coordinator
- End the relationship (the person might be matched with someone else)
- Call or visit the person if they are in the hospital

35

WRAP is a self monitoring system that can help you stay well, feel better, and work on life changes. It includes:

- The Wellness Toolbox
- Daily Maintenance Plan
- Identifying Triggers and an Action Plan
- Identifying Early Warning Signs and an Action Plan
- Signs that Things Are Breaking Down and an Action Plan
- Crisis Planning
- Post Crisis Planning

36

Why Develop a WRAP

WRAP will:

- Help you stay as well as possible
- Help you keep track of difficult feelings and behaviors, and develop action plans to help you feel better.
- Tell others what to do for you when you are feeling so badly that it is more difficult to make decisions and take care of yourself.

37

WRAP can be used as a helpful tool for making life changes like:

- Getting a job or changing jobs
- Taking on more responsibilities
- Getting more education or training
- Changing your living situation
- Moving
- Beginning or leaving an intimate relationship
- Working on relationship issues

38

WRAP can be used to address other life issues like:

- Chronic or acute illness
- Addictions
- Breaking bad habits
- Losing weight
- Caring for an ill or elderly family member
- Trying out new interests

39

Who develops your WRAP

There is only one person who can develop your WRAP — YOU. You, and only you, decide:

- If you want to write one
- How much time it takes you to do it
- When you want to do it
- What you want and don't want in it
- Which parts you want to do
- Who you want, if anyone, to help you with it
- How you use it
- Who you show it to
- Where you keep it
- Who has copies of your crisis plan

40

Helping in the Community Links Relationship

While traditional mental health services are becoming more collaborative, providers sometimes take power away from the person who is receiving services by:

- Diagnosing and labeling people
- Making predictions about their future
- Telling people they have a chemical imbalance
- Ignoring issues related to trauma and abuse

41

- Analyzing and judging people's feelings, behaviors and experiences
- Telling people to avoid taking risks
- Telling people they will need to take medication for the rest of their lives
- Taking away hope for recovery and for the future
- Making decisions about treatment without input from the person involved
- Keeping chart notes
- Reporting to other clinicians
- Avoiding sharing details of their own lives

42

In Community Links, people will be encouraged to reclaim their power by:

- sharing responsibility for the relationship
- talking about what hasn't worked in the past and deciding how to do it differently
- talking in advance about how to keep the connection strong and handling difficult situations (WRAP for Community Links)
- looking at things and situations in many different ways

43

- being willing to change ways of thinking, being and the way you do things
- sharing experiences to strengthen connections, create trust and build hope
- considering the effects of trauma and abuse on people's self-concept and relationships
- supporting and challenging each other to take risks, grow and change.
- validating people's feelings, behaviors and experiences

44

Building Trusting and Mutually Supportive Relationships

- Having a commitment to share feelings and work through difficult issues
- Negotiating difficult issues
- Validation
- Avoiding categorizing, judging and evaluation
- Being honest about what you can and can't do, and about what makes you feel uncomfortable
- Being respectful with each other
- Listening closely to what the other person is saying
- Taking risks with each other
- Sharing strengths and vulnerabilities
- Patience
- Being there for each there even when the going is rough
- Asking for help when we need it
- Being clear about boundaries
- Being willing to be uncomfortable

45

First Contact

Be aware that you may both be nervous or uneasy, even though you have met before. Get together in a place that is comfortable for both of you, a place you arranged in your meeting with the program coordinator.

You can discuss:

- What each of you knows about Community Links
- Times when connections with others have helped you get back on your feet
- Times when you perceived yourself one way, as a mental patient or as an incompetent person, changed that view to a positive one, and how that changed your life

46

- Strengths—you may need to point out the person's strengths, like courage and persistence
- How the relationship can be mutually beneficial
- Things the two of you could do together

Focus your discussion on life and living, and away from a focus on symptoms and mental illness.

47

Avoid statements like:

- I am going to help you recover from your mental illness.
- I am Bill. I have had schizophrenia for years.
- I am Sally. I don't have a mental illness. Tell me what it is like for you to have a mental illness. Did other people in your family have a mental illness? How long have you had a mental illness?

48

Steps in Self Advocacy

1. Believe in yourself.
2. Know your rights.
3. Decide what you want or what you are working toward.
4. Get the facts.
5. Plan your strategy.
6. Gather your support.
7. Target your efforts.
8. Express yourself clearly.
9. Assert yourself calmly.
10. Be firm and persistent.

49

Getting Together

1. The Community Link and the person they link with can use their time together in any way that is agreeable to both of them.
2. If the person is in a treatment facility, arrange to meet them there. When the person has left the facility, meet at a place that is agreeable to both people.
3. At the first session, develop plans for the first few times you will get together. You could also plan for the next meeting only.

50

4. Getting together for two hours, once or twice a week at the convenience of both people is suggested. It can be more or less, depending on what is possible and needed for the Community Links.
5. Meetings can be a mix of social time and time working on issues and activities related to community integration.
6. Be flexible about what will happen at a session. Change plans to best meet needs.

51

Community Links Values

1. Community Links help people to understand that they can take back control of their lives, become independent, have natural supports, that they can do the things they want to do with their lives, and that there is no limit to what they can achieve.
2. Community Links supports self determination, personal responsibility, empowerment and self advocacy.
3. Community Links is a reciprocal relationship in which people treat each other as equals with dignity, compassion, respect and unconditional high regard.

52

4. In Community Links there is acceptance of each person as they are, unique, special individuals, including acceptance of diversity with relation to cultural, ethnic, religious, racial, gender, age, disability and sexual preference issues.

5. Community Links is a totally voluntary program.

6. In Community Links, each person is recognized as the expert on her or himself.

7. Community Links use common language rather than clinical, medical and diagnostic language.

8. Community Links work together to increase mutual understanding, knowledge and promote wellness.

53

9. Community Links validate each other's experiences, including experiences of trauma and abuse.

10. Community Links focus on strengths and away from perceived deficits.

11. Community Links are responsible for their own behavior and do not use symptoms as an excuse for bad behavior.

12. Community Links use honest, direct and respectful communication.

13. Community Links share power and responsibility.

14. Community Links relationships are confidential.

15. Community Links enjoy being and working together.

54

Community Links Evaluation Questions

1. How is this relationship working for you? What do you like about it? What would you like to change? How could we make that change in a way that would work well for both of us?

2. Are you sharing honestly how you feel in Community? If not, why not? How can we make it possible for you to share what you feel in this relationship? Are you asking for what you want and need? If not, why not? How can we make that possible?

55

3. What has changed about the way you think about things since the beginning of Community Links?

4. What do we need to do more of or less of to make sure that Community Links is working for both of us?

5. After you have done this with the person you are working with, both of you can discuss these same questions with the person responsible for program evaluation.

56

C-3.

For use Day 1, Modules 3 and 4

PO Box 301, W. Dummerston, VT 05301 (802) 254–2092 Fax (802) 257–7499

Email: copeland@mentalhealthrecovery.com - web site: www.mentalhealthrecovery.com

Wellness Recovery Action Plan: Personal WRAP Overview

by Mary Ellen Copeland

This handout is a guide to developing a Wellness Recovery Action Plan, a structured system for helping yourself to feel better, to stay well, to improve the quality of your life and to work toward achieving your goals and dreams. It was developed by a group of peers in northern Vermont. It can be used by people to develop their own WRAP, or by people who are helping others to develop Wellness Recovery Action Plans. There are books, articles, audio, and video tapes on how to develop a WRAP. For further information on developing a WRAP and to purchase related resources, go to the website www.mentalhealthrecovery.com or contact Mary Ellen Copeland.

What does WRAP include

WRAP includes the following sections:

- Wellness Toolbox
- Daily Maintenance Plan

- Identifying Triggers and an Action Plan
- Identifying Early Warning Signs and an Action Plan
- Signs that Things Are Breaking Down and an Action Plan
- Crisis Planning
- Post Crisis Planning

Why develop a WRAP

WRAP can:

1. help you stay as well as possible,
2. help you keep track of difficult feelings and behaviors, and develop action plans to help you feel better.
3. tell others what to do for you when you are feeling so badly that you can't make decisions, take care of yourself and keep yourself safe.

WRAP has many additional uses. You can use WRAP as a tool to help ensure your success if you are planning changes in your life like:

Getting a job or changing jobs

Increasing your work hours

Taking on more responsibilities

Getting more education or training

Leaving supported housing

Moving

Beginning or leaving a close relationship

Working on relationship issues

Having a child

You can also use WRAP to address other life issues like:

Chronic or acute illness

Addictions

Breaking bad habits

Losing weight

Caring for an ill or elderly family member

Trying out new interests

Who develops your WRAP

There is only one person who can develop your WRAP—YOU. You, and only you, decide:

If you want to write one

How much time it takes you to do it

When you want to do it

What you want and don't want in it

Which parts you want to do

Who you want, if anyone, to help you with it

How you use it

Who you show it to

Where you keep it

Who has copies of your crisis plan or advance directive

Another person can assist and support a person in this process if the person developing the plan wants their help. The person who develops the plan can choose to share it with the people of their choice, but again, this is never required.

WRAP is totally self determined. If it is not self determined, it is not WRAP. The Plan must be developed by the person who will be using it, when they decide the time is right to develop one. A Wellness Recovery Action Plan must never be required.

Getting Started

Most people use a three ring binder with tabs to develop their WRAP. However, there are many other ways it can be done. It could be developed using any kind of a notebook or copies of WRAP forms. It could be developed on a computer. A person could tape record their WRAP. They could use pictures or symbols rather than words. As you learn about WRAP, you may be able to think of other ways it could be developed that better meet your needs.

Wellness Toolbox

Identify and list all the tools and strategies you have found to be effective in helping you to stay well and in relieving symptoms when they come up. In addition, write possible new skills and strategies you have learned about through this workshop, from supporters and care providers, or through the books listed above. Some of these tools include addressing things like dietary needs, exercise, relaxation exercises, journaling, doing something fun or creative, getting outdoor light, medications, getting support, peer counseling and using spiritual resources. You could put this list in the front of your binder or keep it in a safe place so you can easily refer to it and add new things to your list.

Section 1. ***Daily Maintenance List***

If you are using a binder, on the first tab write "Daily Maintenance List." Insert it in the binder followed by several sheets of filler paper. Make adaptations if you are doing this another way.

On the first page, in list form, describe yourself when you are feeling alright, using words like happy, energetic, competent, capable, introverted, quiet, resourceful, etc.

On the next page make a list of things you need to do for yourself every day to keep yourself feeling alright, like eating three healthy meals, drinking plenty of water, getting outside exercise, and doing relaxation exercises. By doing these things every day you can often keep yourself feeling well.

On the next page, make a reminder list for things you *might* need to do, like buy some groceries, call your doctor, pay some bills, contact a friend, or do something fun. Reading through this list daily helps keep us on track.

Section 2. ***Triggers***

Triggers are external events or circumstances that, if they happen, may make you feel uncomfortable. These are normal reactions to events in our lives, but if we don't respond to them and deal with them in some way, we may notice that we are feeling worse and worse. On the next tab write "Triggers" and put in several sheets of binder paper. On the first page, write down those things that, if they happened, might make you feel worse. They may have triggered or made you feel worse in the past—things like someone being rude to you, the anniversary dates of trauma or loss, not getting enough rest, stress, moving, and illness.

On the next page, write an action plan to use if triggers come up, using the Wellness Toolbox as a guide, to help you through this difficult time. Your action plan might include things like deep breathing exercises, taking a walk, doing some peer counseling and watching a funny video.

Section 3. **Early Warning Signs**

Early warning signs are internal and may be unrelated to reactions to stressful situations. In spite of our best efforts, we may begin to experience early warning signs--subtle signs of change that indicate we may need to take some further action.

On the next tab write “Early Warning Signs.” On the first page of this section, make a list of early warning signs you have noticed, like increased anxiety, headache, aches and pains, negative thoughts and trouble sleeping. On the next page, write an action plan to use if early warning signs come up, using the Wellness Toolbox as a guide—things like getting more exercise, talking to your health care provider, doing extra relaxation exercises, working on a fun project and writing in your journal.

Section 4. **Things are Breaking Down or Getting Worse**

In spite of your best efforts, there may be a time when you feel very uncomfortable, like the situation is serious and even dangerous, but you are still able to take some action on your own behalf. This is a very important time. It is necessary to take immediate action to prevent a much more difficult time.

On the next tab write, "When Things are Breaking Down." Then make a list of the signs that, for you, mean that things have worsened and are close to the crisis stage—like agitation, having a hard time making decisions, crying a lot, wanting to sleep all the time and thinking about using substances.

On the next page, write an action plan to use "When Things are Breaking Down," using the Wellness Toolbox as a guide. You might include things like asking someone to take over your responsibilities for several days, doing several peer counseling exercises each day and asking for around-the-clock support.

Section 5. ***Crisis Planning or Advance Directive***

In spite of our best planning and assertive action, you may find yourself in a difficult situation where others will need to assist and support us until we are feeling better. You may feel as though you are totally out of control.

Writing a crisis plan or Advance Directive when you are well to instruct others about how to care for you when you are not well, keeps you in control even when it seems like things are out of control. Others will know what to do, saving everyone time and frustration, while insuring that your needs will be met. Develop this plan slowly when you are feeling well. You could use the following form.

Crisis Plan or Advance Directive

Name ________________________________ Date ___________

Part 1 What I'm like when I'm feeling well

____

____

____

Part 2 Symptoms and signs

If I have several of the following signs and/or symptoms, my supporters, named on the next page, need to take over responsibility for my care and make decisions in my behalf based on the information in this plan.

____

____

____

____

Part 3 Supporters

If this plan needs to be activated, I want the following people to take over for me.

Name Connection/role Phone number

____

____

____

____

____

I <u>do not</u> want the following people involved in any way in my care or treatment:

Name I don't want them involved because: (optional)

____

____

Settling Disputes Between Supporters

If my supporters disagree on a course of action to be followed, I would like the dispute to be settled in the following way:

____

____

Part 4 Medication

Physician ____________________ Psychiatrist ______________________

Other Health Care Providers

____

____

Pharmacy ___________________ Pharmacist ________________________

Allergies ____

____

Medications and health care preparations I am using

____

____

Medications to be used if necessary

____

____

**Medications and health care preparations to avoid Why?

____

____

Part 5 Treatments

Treatments that help

____

____

Treatments to avoid

____

____

Part 6 Home/Community Care/Respite Center.

If possible, follow the following home and community care plan:

____

____

____

Part 7 Hospital or other treatment facilities.

If I need hospitalization or treatment in a treatment facility, I prefer the following facilities in order of preference

Name Contact Person Phone Number

____

____

____

Avoid using the following hospital or treatment facilities

Name Reason to avoid using

____

____

Part 8 Help from others

Please do the following things that would help reduce my symptoms, make me more comfortable and keep me safe.

____

____

____

____

____

____

I need (name the person) ________________ to (task) ________________________

____

____

I need (name the person) __________________ to (task) ________________________________

____

I need (name the person) __________________ to (task) ________________________________

____

Do not do the following. It won't help and it may even make things worse.

____

____

____

Part 9 Inactivating the Plan

The following signs, lack of symptoms or actions indicate that my supporters no longer need to use this plan.

____

____

____

I developed this plan on (date) _______________ with the help of ___________________

Any plan with a more recent date supersedes this one.

Signed ______________________________ Date __________________

Witness _____________________________ Date __________________

Durable Power of Attorney ____________________________________

Post Crisis Plan

WRAP includes a section on Post Crisis Planning that helps you think about the important time when you are recovering from a very difficult time or crisis. Some of the issues addressed on the post crisis plan forms include:

How I would like to feel when I have recovered from this crisis?

Who will support me through this time?

Having a place to go that is safe and comfortable.

Things I must take care of as soon as I get home.

Things I can ask someone else to do for me.

Things that can wait until I feel better.

Things I need to do for myself every day while I am recovering from crisis.

Things I might need to do every day while I am recovering from this crisis.

Things and people I need to avoid while I am recovering from this crisis.

Signs that I may be beginning to feel worse—anxiety, excessive worry, overeating, sleep disturbances.

Wellness tools I will use if I am starting to feel worse

You can download a complete copy of the Post Crisis Plan from the website www.mentalhealthrecovery.com.

C-4.

To be used Day 1, Module 3

Peer Counseling: A Two-Way Gift Of Attention

by Laura Evans

Do you know what it's like to be listened to really well? ...with full attention, without judgment and without interruption? ...by someone that you know respects and likes you and who you know you can trust? Have you listened to someone else in this way yourself? This sort of listening is the precious gift we give and receive when we do peer counseling.

Of all the many tools that we can use to make our lives what we would like them to be, peer counseling is the one that has meant the most to me. It's helped me grow and change in lots of important ways and is probably the main reason that I'm totally free now of the mental health system, and have been for the past 30 years. I was a third-generation "mental patient," but not anymore.

The free, reciprocal, confidential process of peer counseling is also known as cocounseling, shared listening, support listening, exchange listening and Reevaluation Counseling. Often peer counseling partners will continue to work together for years. The commitment to the process and to each other can really magnify the feelings of safety and healing that are the goal of peer counseling.

Before I say more about the process, I want to mention some of the theory behind it. One of the underlying ideas is that all of us are born good. From birth, we are innately intelligent, curious, and courageous, ready to be closely connected with the people around us and delighted with life. Unfortunately, right from the start, things happen that hurt us, emotionally and physically. Along with the good attention we get as children from our parents and other powerful people in our lives, there are lots of disappointments and hurtful, confusing messages and interactions. All through our lives there are other experiences of hurt and loss as well.

But perhaps worst of all, we are often discouraged from feeling our feelings and given little safety or support to let them out. We're told things like, "Boys don't cry," "It's not nice to say such things about your brother," and "Don't be a baby; there's nothing to be afraid of." So, consciously and unconsciously, we store up unresolved feelings of grief, fear, self-doubt, shame and anger. These can cause us to develop life-long, irrational patterns of thinking and acting that make our lives more difficult than they need to be, and make it hard for us to be as close to other people as we would like.

Now the good news: this emotional muck that has partially obscured lots of our wonderful qualities and capabilities is not made of stone! With support, over time, we can wash away the gunk and let our true selves shine through. Each of us can recover the person we were meant to be. That's what peer counseling is about.

How does the peer-counseling process work? Two people (or a small group) get together to take turns listening to each other, with as few distractions as possible. As we listen, we give our undivided, relaxed, caring attention. The time is shared equally, with each person getting 5 minutes to 1 hour. Often a timer is used to mark the end of a turn. To do really deep work, or if we are in crisis, we need as much time as possible. The amount of time depends on how much we have available and how long we can give good attention. Counseling in person is best, but phone time can be useful too. I have one counseling friend with whom I do five minutes each way of phone time every Tuesday morning, and it's a great way to start my day.

To begin a session, the speaker may share some pleasant observation or experience. The purpose of this is to help them leave their day behind and be present. The session may also end with the listener suggesting a simple, light or humorous exercise to bring the speaker back to the present moment and end on a positive note.

As peer-counseling partners get to know each other better, the sense of safety grows. Gradually both become more relaxed. Whatever feelings come up are discharged through such natural means of healing as talking, laughing, crying, trembling and storming. The release of the distresses frees us to think more clearly and freshly and to act more rationally, for our own good and the good of others. With experience and increasing trust, the process works better and better.

What might a person talk about? People talk about whatever they need to, anything at all, whether personal or work-related. It's a chance to unload upsets—little or huge, in the present or from the past. Or we can use the time to celebrate our successes and think about our dreams and goals and how to work on making them come true. Actually, we don't even have to talk at all. Sometimes we might want to get in touch with feelings another way. For example, we can ask our counseling partner to read aloud a special poem, or to tell us what he likes about us, or to just sit and smile at us with an expression of warm delight while we try to keep eye contact. How the time is used is up to the speaker to decide when it is her turn to have attention paid to her.

The listener helps in these ways: by drawing the person out; by keeping in focus their inherent strengths and goodness; by conveying with posture, facial expression and tone of voice an attitude of respect and affection; by remembering not to give advice or break in with a similar story; and by showing confidence in the speaker's ability to figure out his own solutions to problems.

C-5.

To be used Day 1, Module 4

Building Mutuality into the Relationship using WRAP

If we take what we know about WRAP and translate it into our Community Links relationships, we begin (First Contact) to figure out where we're going together.

Wellness Toolbox

What are some of the things that are crucial to any really mutual relationship? What are some things you do to take care of those relationships?

This might include things like

- ☐ Being honest.
- ☐ Making sure to stay in touch.
- ☐ Sharing your feelings.
- ☐ Making sure that both people are getting their needs met.

Daily Maintenance List

What do your relationships look like when things are going really well? How would you describe the qualities? What might you be doing?

This might include:

- ☐ You feel relaxed together.
- ☐ Both people's opinions are ok.
- ☐ You are learning from each other.
- ☐ You feel strong trust etc.

What are the things you need to do consistently to maintain the relationship?

For example:

- ☐ Checking in with each other regularly.
- ☐ Saying when things aren't feeling right.
- ☐ Asking about each other's interests.
- ☐ Working through conflict.

Triggers

What are some of the things that might upset or stir up trouble in a mutually responsible relationship?

For example:

- ☐ You have a disagreement.
- ☐ One person is really tired.
- ☐ One person feels upset about what the other person has said or done.
- ☐ Outside circumstances (something else in your life is going on that you don't want to share).

Triggers Action Plan

- ☐ Remember to breathe or take a walk.
- ☐ Say that you know you're tired and maybe overreacting.
- ☐ Use good communication skills to say what you heard, and then negotiate what you need.

Early Warning Signs

What might be going on in the relationship if things are starting to get steadily more rocky?

- ☐ People stop being honest with each other.
- ☐ Only talking small talk.
- ☐ Talking behind each other's backs.
- ☐ Taking power.
- ☐ Relinquishing power.

Early Warning Signs Action Plan

What do you need to do to get back on track?

- ☐ Own that you've not been being honest.
- ☐ Be willing to look inside yourself and say what you see/hear.
- ☐ Figure out how you're going to negotiate issues of power/safety.

When things are Breaking Down

What does it look like when things are really falling apart?

- ☐ You are threatening to each other.
- ☐ You stop caring what the other person needs.
- ☐ It becomes all about one person and the other person is burned out.

When things are breaking down Action Plan

- ☐ Go back and look the qualities of what makes our relationship really positive.
- ☐ Talk about power and control and who needs to do what.
- ☐ Call in another person to act as mediator.

C-6.

To be used Day 2, Module 2

Building Trusting and Mutually Supportive Relationships

How do you know when to trust someone? When not to trust?

What do you think might happen in your relationships with people who have learned not to trust their own thoughts and perceptions? What will you do if you find yourself not trusting/believing what someone else is saying?

What might you do to help build a sense of trust with someone who clearly doesn't trust you?

How can you deal with it if someone makes you feel uncomfortable, "pushes your buttons", without having the relationship break down?

How can you and your link share the power in your relationship? How will you avoid having one person be the helper and the other the person who is helped?

How will you respond if the person you are working with says something that scares you like, "I am thinking of ending my life"?

What boundaries will you want to have in your Community Links relationship?

Examples;

- No phone calls after 9 at night.
- Not meeting in each other's homes.
- No loaning or borrowing.
- No asking for money.
- No going in bars.

C-7.

Negotiating the Relationship

1. You're in a coffee shop with the person you are supporting. He/she starts getting really loud and you're afraid you might get thrown out of the restaurant.
2. The person you're working with tells you that you have no idea what you're doing and that he/she would rather be in the hospital where "people are professionals".
3. The person you're working with says that them feeling like this is just too hard and maybe they'd rather just end it.
4. The person you're working with says something that really offends you (for example, makes a racial slur).
5. Every time you show up to do something with the other person, they've been drinking. Alcohol is prohibited on their court order.
6. You've noticed that the person you're working with smells pretty bad most of the time and people in town make faces or walk way around you when you're in town.

C-8.

To use Day 2, Module 4

Steps in Self Advocacy

1. Believe in yourself.

Remind the participants that they are all very wonderful, special, and unique, that they are important and that they deserve all the very best that life has to offer. Provide paper and pens or pencils. Let them take 10 minutes to write down all their positive attributes. Then tell them to carry this paper with them, to reread it every time they are waiting for a few minutes, when they first get up in the morning and before they go to bed at night.

2. Know your rights.

Ask participants to share rights that they are aware of and that are important to them. Use the "Bill of Rights" transparency to remind people of other rights they have and to start a discussion of rights. People sometimes want to reword one of the rights or add new ones to the list. Encourage them to change their handouts as they see fit.

Have available the name, address and phone number of your state's agency of protection and advocacy. Encourage participants to call this number for assistance, advice and support if they feel their rights are being violated.

3. Decide what you want or what you are working toward.

Ask participants to share what they want and what they are working toward.

4. Get the facts.

Give examples of how you have gathered information about something you have needed or wanted, that is, using resource books, the library, health care professionals, a health care organization, etc. For instance, if a person wanted to get a complete thyroid test, they would go to a medical library or resource books to get information that will support their request.

5. Plan your strategy.

Share ways that you have planned your strategy when advocating for yourself. Ask participants for other ideas.

6. Gather your support.

Ask participants to share who their supporters are and how they would use them. Remind them that you will be discussing making and keeping a support system later in the workshop.

7. Target your efforts.

Ask participants who they would target to get the following:

- ☐ a complete thyroid test.
- ☐ further education.
- ☐ safe housing.
- ☐ copies of mental health records.
- ☐ changes in their treatment plan.
- ☐ vocational rehabilitation services.
- ☐ compensation for rights violation in a treatment facility.

8. Express yourself clearly.

9. Assert yourself calmly.

10. Be firm and persistent.

Using the examples listed for Point 7, ask participants to role play advocating for themselves.

For further information, review Chapter 1 in *Living Without Depression and Manic Depression*, "How to Advocate Effectively for Yourself."

C-9.

To be used Day 2, Module 4

Personal Bill of Rights

1. I have the right to ask for what I want.
2. I have the right to say no to requests or demands I can't meet.
3. I have the right to change my mind.
4. I have the right to make mistakes and not have to be perfect.
5. I have the right to follow my own values and standards.
6. I have the right to express all of my feelings, both positive or negative, in a manner that will not harm others.
7. I have the right to say no to anything when I feel I am not ready, it is unsafe, or it violates my values.
8. I have the right to determine my own priorities.
9. I have the right not to be responsible for others' behavior, actions, feelings or problems.
10. I have the right to expect honesty from others.
11. I have the right to feel angry at someone I love and to express this in a responsible manner.
12. I have the right to be uniquely myself.
13. I have the right to feel scared and say "I'm afraid."
14. I have the right to say "I don't know."

15. I have the right to make decisions based on my feelings, beliefs and values.

16. I have the right to my own reality.

17. I have the right to my own needs for personal space and time.

18. I have the right to be playful and frivolous.

19. I have the right to be healthy.

20. I have the right to be in a nonabusive environment.

21. I have the right to make friends and be comfortable around people.

22. I have the right to change and grow.

23. I have the right to have my needs and wants respected by others.

24. I have the right to be treated with dignity and respect.

25. I have the right to grieve.

26. I have the right to a fulfilling sex life.

27. I have the right to be happy.

(Adapted by Mary Ellen Copeland from the *Anxiety and Phobia Workbook*, Edmund J. Bourne, Ph.D., 1990, New Harbinger Publications, Oakland, CA.)

C-10.

To be used Day 3, Module 1

Getting Together

The Community Link and the person they link with can use their time together in any way that is agreeable to both of them. At first, the person may be in a treatment facility. Arrangements should be made to the meet with the person there. When the person has left the facility, they can meet at a place that is agreeable to both people, usually the living space of the person they are supporting.

The Community Link works with the person requesting services to develop plans for the first few times they get together. They can plan the other meetings as they go along, and find out what is most helpful. Two hours, once or twice a week at the convenience of both people is suggested. There are suggestions here for 16 meetings. However, they could have more or less meetings. They can also do more or less in each session. Meetings can be a mix of social time and time working on issues and activities related to community integration.

The Community Link and the person they are matched with can use the form at the end of this section to set up their schedule and to write things they may want to do or topics they may want to cover. The Community Link needs be flexible about what will be done at a session to best meet the need of the person they are matched with.

Include social and fun activities as often as both of you would like to do so. Get out into the community. Some ideas for social time and fun activities include:

playing games,

watching a video,

going for a walk,

cooking together,

grocery shopping,

shopping or window shopping,

going to a thrift shop or tag sale,

going somewhere of mutual interest like the mall or to a park,

going to an art exhibit or a concert,

attending a community event,

going to a snack shop for coffee or lunch, etc.

spending time talking about life,

sharing some jokes and having a good time.

List other ideas of possible thing you might do together that are social and/or fun:

1.

2.

3.

4.

Reminder notes of meetings and things to do or work on can be written or tape-recorded.

You may want to spend time at each meeting (and sometimes this might be all of the time), talking about meeting specific needs in the community that the person has right now.

Following are suggestions for things that might be done at each meeting. They are only suggestions. You and the person you are working with can decide how you want to use your time together.

Meeting 1—Find out how a person would like to keep track of what they are doing. They can decide on a binder with binder paper, a spiral notebook, a bound notebook, a file envelope, tapes or CD's. They can also decide on the Wellness Recovery Action Plan Resource they want to work with. The resource choices include: A copy of the book, Wellness Recovery Action Plan, the audio cd WRAP Step by Step, or WRAP Software for computers. These supplies and resources are available through the sponsoring agency or the training facilitators. While the materials are not as comprehensive or accessible for some people, the program can be implemented by using resources downloaded from the website at www.mentalhealthrecovery.com. Binders and other supplies might be donated. People in the program could purchase their own supplies if necessary.

Introductions—people take turns asking the other person questions that they feel will help them know the other person better. Each person can choose to not answer. Possible questions include:

What is your favorite color?

If you could live anyplace in the world, where would you live?

Where was the best place you ever lived? What did you like about it?

What are your favorite things to do?

What are you really good at?

Describe the best time you ever had in your whole life?

Spend 5 minutes each sharing goals and dreams, without interruption from the other.

Discuss what the person feels they need in order to make a successful transition to the community—you could make a list of these or tape record them.

Meeting 2—Give the person their copy of the book, tape, or computer disk that describes the Wellness Recovery Action Plan. This is theirs to keep. Tell them what the program is about. Review WRAP on the CD or using the handout (Appendix C-3).

Begin building a Wellness Toolbox by discussing and listing the personal resources and strengths that a person has to use in their recovery and facilitate their integration into the community. These could include things like:

Specific skills like carpentry, computer technology, cooking, mathematics, knitting.

Attributes like patient, compassionate, thoughtful, smart, humorous.

People they like.

Things they like to do—fishing, sewing, exercising.

Meeting 3—Continue to work on the Wellness Toolbox. What are other things they could put in their Wellness Toolbox—refer to the lists in the handouts from the training that you can give to the person.

Identify resources in the Community that could be used to facilitate integration into the community and recovery—use lists generated at the training. Ask the person to share other resources they know about. Talk about how these resources could be used. Help them start to develop their own binder of resources—this is separate from the WRAP binder. Are there places they would like to go with you in the community?

Help the person describe what they are like when they feel well. Single words or short sentences are fine. Even pictures from magazines or drawings will work out well. If you have a digital camera and it is ok with the person, you could take their picture and bring them a copy next time to put on the first page of their Wellness Recovery Action Plan. If possible, they can begin to put their materials into the binder or the organizational system they have chosen.

If the person is preparing to leave the facility, ask them one thing they need when they leave. Then problem solve how they could meet that need. Discuss any tasks that need to be made like making phone calls and talk about who will do these things. The Community Link could coach the person about making calls or go with them to appointments.

Meeting 4—Develop a Daily Maintenance Plan: a list of things the person feels they need to do every day to feel as well as possible (they can use things from the wellness toolbox for this list). Also develop a list of things that a person doesn't need to do every day but might need to do occasionally. Refer to the resources for ideas.

These lists can be tape-recorded, included in the binder or the envelope file or organized and stored any way that the person wishes.

Meeting 5—Discuss the following questions.

What does the community have to offer?

What are your rights in the community? How do you make sure your rights are respected? How do you respond if your rights are not respected? Is this helpful? If not, are there other ways that this could be handled that might be more helpful?

What are your responsibilities in the community? How did you make sure you fulfill these responsibilities? Are there some of these responsibilities that you have been neglecting? If so, what could you do about it?

What might upset you in the community? Is there anything you can do to keep this from happening? If it happens, how do you respond? Would another way of responding be more helpful? Is so, what would that be? Can you identify any tools that would help?

What kinds of things are upsetting to you? Make a list of these things for the Triggers section of your binder. If you get upset what happens? Are there any tools you could use to help yourself feel better and avoid trouble if you are upset? If so, what are they? How and when would you use them? This is the Action Plan that you can use when you are upset.

What places would you like to go in the community? Can you go there? If not, why not? How could we make it safe and comfortable for you to go there? Could we go there together? If so, when would you like to do that?

Meeting 6—Discuss the following questions

Do you ever notice that you don't feel quite right? What does that feel like for you? List these things for the Early Warning Signs section of your binder. Are there some tools in our Wellness Toolbox that might help you to feel better when you don't feel quite right? Make a list of them to include in your binder.

Is there a place in the community where you think you could meet some new friends? What would it be like to go there? Could we go there together? Are there other such places? Is there anything we should talk about that might make it easier for you to go?

Meeting 7—How do you know when you are feeling really badly? Make a list of things that let you know you are feeling really badly. List the Wellness Tools can you use to help yourself feel better during these times. Think about simple things that make you feel good.

Meeting 8—Most of us have had some very difficult times in our lives, times that may be referred to as a crisis. You may want to develop a document that tells others how to help you in these times so that they help you to get through this time and they don't make things worse. Use the form in Appendix C-3, working through each section.

Meeting 9—Continue working on the Advance Directive or Crisis Plan, working through each section together. When the Advance Directive is complete the two of you may want to take it to a Legal Aid lawyer to have them review and sign it.

How can you use the Advance Directive or Crisis Plan to keep your connections in the community strong? Who do you want to give copies of your Advance Directive? Is this something we could do together? Would you like to set up a time to meet with some of these people? How could we do that?

Meeting 10—After you have had a difficult time, it is sometimes difficult to get over the effects of the hard time. Discuss this situation and respond to some of the questions in the post crisis plan.

Meeting 11–14—Continue working together on WRAP or review it and talk about how it is working.

Discuss issues related to developing Recovery Security and make action plans—

Finances

Getting groceries

Food

Clothes

A place to live

Transportation

Friends

Family

Health care

Meeting 15—Continue working together on WRAP, developing resources and supports in the community, building Recovery Security and sharing social and fun activities.

If this is so, discuss that the next time will be your last time together. Ask them what they need to make that easier. Plan a good-bye celebration, honoring yourselves for all the good work you have done together. Discuss the possibility of ongoing contact after the project ends.

Meeting 16—Review the work you have done together. Celebrate.

C-11.

To be used Day 3, Module 1

Capacity Inventory-Ideas for Focus

Leisure Skills

_______ Writing creatively and/or poetry

_______ Inventing Games

_______ Stretching a tight budget

_______ Drawing/painting

_______ Sculpting

_______ Fishing

_______Hiking

_______Camping

_______Sailing/boating

_______Bicycling

_______Singing

_______Playing an instrument

_______Acting

_______Dancing

_______Mowing lawns

_______Planting and caring for gardens

_______Pruning trees and shrubs

_______Cleaning swimming pools

_______Floor sanding or stripping

_______Wood stripping/refinishing

_______Other

General skills

_______Upholstering

_______Sewing

_______Crocheting or knitting

_______Moving furniture or equipment

_______Managing property

_______Assisting in a classroom

_______Hair cutting/styling

_______Taking phone surveys

_______Repairing jewelry or watches

Food Preparation Skills

_______Catering

_______Serving food to large groups

_______Cooking for large groups

_______Washing dishes for large groups

_______Preparing commercial food

_______ Bartending

_______Butchering

_______Baking

Transportation

_______ Driving a car or taxi

_______ Driving a bus or large van

_______ Driving a tractor trailer

_______ Driving a commercial truck

_______ Hauling

_______ Driving a delivery truck

_______ Operating farm equipment

Operation and Repair

_______ Repairing radios, TV's, VCR's

_______ Repairing small appliances

_______ Repairing cars, trucks, busses

_______ Doing automotive body work

_______ Repairing large appliances

_______ Repairing heating systems

_______ Using a forklift

_______ Operating a dump truck

_______ Operating a crane

_______ Assembling machinery

Supervision Skills

_______Writing reports

_______ Filling out forms

_______ Planning work schedules

_______ Directing projects

_______ Making a budget

_______ Keeping records of activities

_______ Interviewing

Sales

_______ Operating cash register

_______ Selling—wholesale

_______ Selling—retail

_______ Selling of services

_______ Selling door to door

_______ Selling by phone

_______ Selling by mail

People skills

_______ Caring for people who are elderly

_______ Caring for people with disabilities

_______ Caring for people who are sick

_______ Caring for children

_______ Reading to children

_______ Playing games with children

_______ Taking children on field trips

_______ Ushering at major events

Office Skills

_______ Typing

_______Running an adding machine

_______Filing

_______Answering phones

_______Writing business letters

_______Operating Switchboard

_______Taking notes in shorthand

_______Bookkeeping

_______Transcribing

_______Word Processing

_______Using Internet skills

Construction Maintenance and Repair

_______Painting

_______Wallpapering

_______Repairing or changing locks

_______Tiling

_______Taping and mudding drywall

_______Plumbing

_______Repairing electrical components

_______Pointing brickwork and masonry

_______Welding

_______Building

_______Roofing

_______Washing windows

_______Waxing or mopping floors

_______Cleaning carpets

_______Cleaning—general household

C-12.

Community Links Scheduling Form

To be used Day 3, Module 1

Community Link (name)

Date	Time	Place	Plan

C-13.

To be used Day 3, Module 2

Values in Action

1. You've been working on a WRAP plan with the person you're linked with. It has been going very well until this week when the person tells you he/she thinks this is a waste of time and that he/she doesn't want to work on it anymore. You say, "But you're so close…if we just finish this today, you'll see how much better it will make you feel."
2. The person you're working with seems more tired and uninterested than usual. You ask if he/she has been taking his/her medications.
3. When you go to pick up the person you're working with one of the group home staff ask you how the person seems to be doing. You say, "Thanks for asking, I'll go get (name of person) and maybe he/she can share with us what he/she thinks about Community Links."
4. The person you're working with does something that makes you really uncomfortable but you're afraid you'll hurt his/her feelings if you say something. You act like nothing is wrong but then go back to the program coordinator and say that you no longer want to work with this person.
5. The person you're working with has really been enjoying your company. He/she wants to spend more time with you. Your response is that the hours set up for Community Links are nonnegotiable.

C-14.

To be used Day 3, Module 21.

Community Links Evaluation Questions

1. How is this relationship working for you? What do you like about it? What would you like to change? How could we make that change in a way that would work well for both of us?
2. Are you sharing honestly how you feel in the Community Links relationship? If not, why not? How can we make it possible for you to share what you feel in this relationship? Are you asking for what you want and need? If not, why not? How can we make that possible?
3. What has changed about the way you think about things since the beginning of Community Links?
4. What do we need to do more of or less of to make sure that Community Links is working for both of us?

After you have done this with the person you are working with, both of you can discuss these same questions with the person responsible for program evaluation.

D. Certificate

____

Has successfully completed the training

Community Links:

Pathways to Reconnection and Recovery

Training Leader ______________________ Training Leader _______________________

Date ___________

E.

Resources List

It would be helpful if the training leaders had copies of the following books. Some of the Community Links and the people they are working with may also want copies.

Copeland, M. E. (2000). *Winning against relapse.* Brattleboro, VT: Peach Press.

This book describes using the Wellness Recovery Action Planning system in different settings and to meet various needs.

Copeland, M. E. (2002). *Wellness recovery action plan.* Brattleboro, VT: Peach Press.

Known as the "Little Red WRAP Book," this book takes people through the process of developing their own Wellness Recovery Action Plan.

Copeland, M.E., & S. Mead. (2004). *WRAP and peer support: Personal, group and program development.* Brattleboro, VT: Peach Press.

This book gives an in-depth description of using Wellness Recovery Action Planning in peer relationships and organizations.

The Community Links program would benefit from having copies of the following resources available for use by everyone in the program.

Copeland, M. E. (2001). *The creating wellness series* [Video series]. Boston: Mental Illness Education Project.

This video series introduces people to the key concepts of mental health recovery, the specifics of developing a Wellness Toolbox and the step-by-step process of developing a Wellness Recovery Action Plan.

Copeland, M. E. (1994). *Living without depression and manic depression.* Oakland, CA: New Harbinger.

This workbook is for people who have been working on their recovery and are ready to move ahead more quickly.

Copeland, M. E. (1999). *The loneliness workbook.* Oakland, CA: New Harbinger.

This workbook takes people through the various steps necessary to develop a circle of friends, acquaintances and supporters.

Copeland, M. E. (2001). *The depression workbook: A guide for living with depression and manic depression* (2nd ed., Vol. 1). Oakland, CA: New Harbinger.

This is a beginning workbook for people who are starting to explore mental health recovery.

Patton, M. Q. (2001). *Qualitative research and evaluation methods.* Thousand Oaks, CA: Sage.

Patton's comprehensive work will guide the Program Coordinator and Working Committee through the process of studying and evaluating their program.

Order Form:

Intentional Peer Support: An Alternative Approach
Shery Mead, MSW.......................... $30 US

- ($25 for 6 or more copies)

Shipping and Handling: $2.50/ book

Order form

Name: ______________________________

Address______________________________

____

____

Title	Number	Cost	S/H

TOTAL ____________________

Please contact Shery Mead at 603-469-3577 (phone and fax) or shery@mentalhealthpeers.com to order books or articles. Remit payment to Shery Mead 302 Bean Rd Plainfield, NH 03781

Self-Help Resources by Mary Ellen Copeland

Books

The Depression Workbook: A Guide to Living with Depression and Manic Depression Second Edition ______ copies at $19.95

Fibromyalgia and Chronic Myofascial Pain Syndrome: A Survival Manual with Devin Starlanyl........ ______ copies at $19.95

Healing the Trauma of Abuse: A Women's Workbook with Maxine Harris, Ph.D .... ______ copies at $24.95

Living Without Depression and Manic Depression: A Guide to Maintaining Mood Stability.............. ______ copies at $21.95

The Loneliness Workbook .... ______ copies at $18.95

Recovering from Depression: A Workbook for Teens with Stuart Copans, MD...................................... ______ copies at $24.95

The Worry Control Workbook .... ______ copies at $16.95

WRAP: Wellness Recovery Action Plan .... ______ copies at $10.00

WRAP: Wellness Recovery Action Plan for People with Dual Diagnosis .... ______ copies at $10.00

Plan de Acción para la Recuperación del Bienestar WRAP-Spanish Version .... ______ copies at $10.00

Quantity pricing for WRAP books: 1-9 copies - $10 each • 10-99 copies - $8 each • 100+ copies - $7 each
WRAP shipping: $4 for one WRAP book, plus $0.50 for each additional copy

WRAP Software CD with printable worksheets and instructions, contains both adult & teen versions....... ______ copies at $19.95

WRAP and Peer Support: Personal, Group & Program Development with Shery Mead....................... ______ copies at $40.00

Quantity pricing for WRAP and Peer Support: 1-4 copies - $40 • 5-9 copies - $35 • 10-49 copies - $30 • 50+ copies - $25

Winning Against Relapse: A Workbook of Action Plans for Recurring Health & Emotional Problems
Expanded version of WRAP with suggestions for group work .... ______ copies at $16.95

Facilitator Manual: Mental Health Recovery including WRAP with CD-ROM of transparencies,
one WRAP book, and complete instructions for teaching WRAP.. ______ copies at $129.00

Quantity pricing for Facilitator Manuals: 1-11 copies - $129 each • 12+ copies - $110 each
Manual shipping: $8 for one Manual, plus $5 for each additional copy

Advanced Mental Health Recovery Manual: Leading a WRAP Facilitator Training .... ______ copies at $60.00

Videos and Audio CDs

Creating Wellness Workshop Video Series produced by Mental Illness Education Project

Key Concepts for Mental Health video .... ______ copies at $39.95

The Wellness Toolbox video .... ______ copies at $39.95

Developing a Wellness Recovery Action Plan video .... ______ copies at $39.95

Wellness Tools audio CD.. ______ copies at $19.95

WRAP: Step-by-Step audio CD... ______ copies at $19.95

Subtotal: $ ______________

Shipping/Handling*: $4.00 for first item, +$1.00 for each additional item: $______________
*Please use special shipping rates listed above for multiple WRAP books and Facilitator Manuals

Total amount due: $______________

Name: ____

Organization (if applicable): ______________________________________

Address: ____

City/State: __________________________________ Zip: ______________

Phone: ______________________ E-mail: __________________________

Make checks payable to: Mary Ellen Copeland

( ) MasterCard ( ) Visa Card #: ______________________________ Expires: ________

Mail order to: Mary Ellen Copeland, P.O. Box 301, West Dummerston, VT 05357-0301

Phone (802) 425-3660 ♦ FAX (802) 425-5580 ♦ books@mentalhealthrecovery.com ♦ www.mentalhealthrecovery.com

06/06